Real Estate Investing: Rental Property + Flipping Houses (2 Manuscripts)

Includes Wholesaling Homes, Passive Income, Apartment Buying & Selling, Money Management, and Financial Freedom Strategies

James Connor

professional before attempting any techniques outlined in this book.

By reading this document, the reader agrees that under no circumstances is the author responsible for any losses, direct or indirect, which are incurred as a result of the use of information contained within this document, including, but not limited to, — errors, omissions, or inaccuracies.

Table of Contents

Rental Property

Introduction *2*

Chapter 1: Rental Property 101 .... *4*

Pros and Cons of Rental Property Investing...... 4

Direct income..4

Appreciation of the property 5

Sweat equity...5

Tax benefits 6

Identify Your Investment Goals 8

Principles of Success 9

Learn to manage efficiently 10

Increasing your income...11

Reduce the expenses 12

The property matters 12

Tenants..13

Investing Strategies 13

Type of Investment 15

Single-family units 15

Multi-residential units 16

Real Estate Investment Team...........................17

Real estate agents...17

Property manager 19

Chapter 2: Sample Plans 22

Develop a Business Plan 22
Step one: Setting your passive income goals........24
Step two: Selecting your market............................24
Step three: Estimating all your expenses and the
sources of finance 25
Step four: Marketing strategies.............................27
Step five: Managing the rental property...............28

Chapter 3: How to Find Rental Properties 30

Different Sources to Consider 30
Through your network...30
Find properties online 32
Realtors can be helpful..32
Don't overlook the print media 32
Auctions...33

Steps for Choosing an Investment Property.....34
Appreciation of the rental property.......................36
Return rate...37
Calculate the capitalization rate.............................38
1% Rule 38

Chapter 4: Analyzing a Rental Property............... 39

The Big Picture...39
Income matters..39
Price appreciation...40
Property price and inflation....................................40

Property is localized 41

Specific Steps to Follow 41
Calculate the annual gross yield..........................41
Compare the gross rental yield to the risk-free rate
....42
Calculate the annual net rent yield 42
Compare the net rental yield to the risk-free rate 43
Price to earnings ratio 43
Property price and rental expectations forecast...44
Various situations 44
Taxes and depreciation 45

Cash Flow Analysis 45
Total income 46
Total expenses...47

Cash on Cash Return on Investment 49

Cash Flow using the 50% rule 50

Chapter 5: Location of The Property 52

Big-picture Location Criteria 52
Jobs and economics 53
Population growth...54
Price-rent ratio 55

Small-scale Location Criteria 55
Convenience..56
Romance 56
Crime rates and safety...58
School districts..59

Public transport 59

Neighborhood covenants 60

Local laws 61

Barriers to supply 63

Chapter 6: Rental Property Management Strategies
.... **65**

Types of Management Strategies **65**

Do-It-Yourself Approach 65

Half and Half Approach 67

Outsourcing Everything 69

Steps of Self-Management **70**

The correct rent 71

Automate the process 71

Learn the landlord-tenant laws 72

Diligent screening 73

Legal agreement 73

Property maintenance 74

Performing regular inspections 74

Insurance is a must 75

Tax time 75

Network 76

Chapter 7: Financing Options **77**

House Hacking **78**

Seller Financing **79**

Assuming the Seller's Mortgage **80**

Negotiating a Second Mortgage 81

Collateral-Based Lending............................... 81

Partners... 82

Credit Cards.. 83

HELOCs 84

Other Options 86

Saving your tax returns 87
Set aside part of your payroll for investment 88
Living modestly... 88
Additional sources of income 89

Chapter 8: Exit Strategies *90*

Types of Exit Strategies 92

Sell.. 93
Own outright.. 94
Refinancing.. 95
HELOC 95
Staying put 96

Chapter 9: Stages of a Screening Process *97*

First Contact... 98

When to start screening? 99
Questions to include 99

Show the Property 102

Tips to follow.. 103
Red flags to watch out for............................ 104
Rental Applications 106

Accept and Reject **109**

Credit report 111

Sign the Rental Agreement **112**

Reviewing the rental agreement 112

Security deposit, first month's rent, and the move-
in fees 114

Setting a deadline 115

Chapter 10: Increase Tenant Retention Rate *117*

Understand the Market **118**

List of Improvements **119**

Referral Program **120**

Screening is Important **120**

Maintain Reference Files **121**

Raise the Rent **122**

Pick up the Phone and Call **123**

Don't Barge into the Property **124**

Prioritize the Responsiveness **124**

Sending Holiday Cards **125**

Pruning is a Must **125**

Chapter 11: Mistakes to Avoid *127*

**Mistakes to Avoid while Buying a Rental
Property** **127**

Concentrating only on appreciation 128

A watertight contract 129

Hiring a third-party... 129

Lack of proper insurance... 130

Too many properties.. 131

Common Mistakes Rental Property Owners Make **132**

Don't try to do everything by yourself................ 133

Only a specific service provider 133

Hiring a real estate agent 134

Charging the wrong rent... 135

Improper insurance 135

Clear rules 135

Unhealthy relationships 136

Repairs and maintenance.. 136

Legal Mistakes to Avoid....................................... 137

Discriminating queries 137

Failure to disclose 138

Illegal elements in the rental deed...................... 138

Provide a safe environment 139

Refusing to make repairs 139

Violating the tenant's right to privacy 140

Eviction rules 140

Withholding the security deposits....................... 141

Deal with abandoned property............................. 141

Inadequate insurance.. 142

Conclusion *143*

Flipping Houses

Introduction *146*

Chapter 1: Basic Concepts *148*

House Flipping: What is it? 148

Wholesale Flipping 148

Rehabbing 149

How Does House Flipping Work? 150

How Much Can You Make Flipping? 152

Taxes You Need to Pay as A Home Flipper ... 153

Ordinary Income Tax Implications When
Flipping Properties 154

When is Capital Gains Tax Applicable to House
Flipping? 155

Does Flipping Still Work in Today's Market? . 155

Chapter 2: The Renovating/Rehab Process *160*

Appraise the Investment Property 160

Make a Checklist 161

Create a Budget 162

Locate The Appropriate Contractor 162

Get the Needed Permits 163

Rehabbing the Property 164

Begin the Cleanup Phase 164

Begin with Enhancements to The Interior 165

Enhance the Exterior.. 165

Finalizing Stage... **166**

Chapter 3: Get Your Financing in Place............. *167*

Getting Financing **168**

**Things to Put in Place Before You Apply for A
House Flipping Loan**...................................... **168**
Develop a Business Plan for Every Flip 169
Get Accurate Estimates of All Costs of
Renovation 170
Develop Your Network... 171

Ways to Get Financing **171**
Bank Financing 172
Personal Loans.. 172
Line of Credit... 173
Hard Money Loan 174
Loan from Family and Friends............................ 175
Look for a Financing Partner 176
Real Estate Crowdfunding Sites 177
401(k) Financing 177

Your Financial Inventory **178**
Credit Score/Credit History 179
Your Earnings... 179
Your Resources... 180
Debt.. 181
Familiarity with Investing..................................... 181

Chapter 4: Locate Your Agent(s)....................... *183*

Is Your Housing Market Suitable for Flipping Houses?..184

An Agent Can Locate the Appropriate House for You..184

An Agent Offers You Market-Driving Tips When Remodeling 186

An Agent Offers You Advise On When-to-Sell187

What Kind of Agent Should You Choose?.......188

Dual Agents 189

How to Choose a House Flipping...................191

Experience..191

Has Time for You...192

Devoted to their Job..193

Inspired by Relationships......................................193

Capable of Learning...194

How to Get Your Real Estate License 194

What Can You Use a Real Estate License for?196

Is it Compulsory to get a Real Estate License to Flip Homes? 196

Benefits of Having Your Real Estate License as A Rehabber 197

Chapter 5: Where You Should Buy?....................200

How to Choose the Right Real Estate Farm Area 200

Choose a Farm Area Close to Home..................201

Investigate Your Farm Area.................................. 203

Pick a Farm Area with Clear Boundaries........... 205

Ensure Your Farming Area Is the Appropriate

Size.. 206

Check your Farm Area's Numbers 206

Piecing It All Together....................................208

How to Develop Authority in Your Farm Area

for Real Estate 209

Direct Mail.. 209

Knocking on Doors 210

Door Hangers 210

Facebook Advertising... 211

Take Part in Online Local Forums 211

Meetup Groups and Local Events....................... 212

Get Your Website Ranked on Google Using Local

Search Terms... 212

Chapter 6: Who Should You Buy From? 214

Buying from Owners with Equity 214

Buying from Absentee Owners with Equity ... 215

Buying from Owners Without Equity 216

Buying Foreclosures at Auction...................... 217

Buying (REO) Bank-Owned Foreclosures..... 217

Choosing the Best Option for You.................. 218

Chapter 7: How to Locate the Best Deals 220

Use the MLS.. 220

Become a Part of a Real Estate Investment Group 221
Search for Auctions 222
Talk to Wholesalers 223
Use Classifieds...223
Find an Agent...224
Use a Short Sale..225
Use REO 226
Seller Direct..226
Take a Drive Around...227
Check The Internet for Listings..........................227

Chapter 8: What is the Financial Formula for Flipping Homes?..229

ARV or After Repair Value Formula 229

70% Rule Formula 230

Maximum Buying Price 230

Expected Return on Investment 231

The Formula for Offer Price...........................231

Chapter 9: How to Make Offers...........................232

Crafting a Good Offer 232
Run a Comparative Market Analysis (CMA) 232
Consider Market Indicators...................................233
Determine The Motivation of the Seller 234
Learn About Other Offers on the Home..........235

Get a Pre-Approval Letter if it Is a Financed Deal
.... 236

Make A Larger Down Payment........................... 236

Get an Attorney to Analyze the Offer 236

Engaging in Negotiations....................................237

Open negotiations 237

Start your bid low 237

Stay Calm 238

Play Hard to Get... 238

Reach Out to Sellers Directly 238

Sealed Bids 239

Holding Deposits 239

Seller Counteroffers and Responses.................240

Agreeing to The Terms... 241

Rejecting/Refusing The Terms 241

Make a Counteroffer... 241

Chapter 10: Doing Your Due Diligence.............243

The Legal Due Diligence...................................243

Due Diligence Tasks..243

Do Your Homework.. 244

Go Through the Title History 245

Take a Look at Homeowners Association
Restrictions and Covenants.................................. 246

Inspect The Property 247

Preparing for The Inspection of a Property....248

What a Home Inspection May Not Entail 249

General Home Inspection 251
(WDO) Wood-Destroying Organisms Inspection
....251
Lead-Based Paint Inspection.................................252
Radon Gas Inspection...252

Run Your Numbers Once More 254

Steps to Take if the Numbers Are Not Right 254
Request for a Reduction in Price 255
Walk Away from The Deal......................................256

Chapter 11: Hiring Contractors 257

What Type of Contractor Do You Need? 258

Finding the Right Contractor for Your Project
... 259

Places to Find Your Contractor 260
Referrals from Real Estate Investment Clubs
(REIC) 260
Ask Subcontractors...260
Check Out Your Farm Area....................................261
Check Hardware Stores...261
Check Online..261

Questions to Ask Before You Hire a Contractor
... 262
Have You Worked for Someone Similar? 263
How Long Have You Been in This Job?............263

Do You Work Alone? 263

Is There Any Area You Don't Work On? 264

Are You Presently Working On Any Project? .. 264

Do You Have the Required License? 264

Do You Have Insurance? 265

**Signs to Look Out for When Choosing a
Contractor 265**

Get Numerous Bids 268

Analyze the Job 269

What to Do About an Unreliable Contractor .. 269

Understand Your Options of Payment 270

Draw Up a Written Contract 271

After Hiring a Contractor 273

Keep detailed records 273

Release Payments Wisely 274

Be Aware of the Limit for the Final Bill 274

Know When You Can Deny Payment 274

Take Advantage of a Sign-Off Checklist 275

Chapter 12: Managing Your Rehab 276

Make a detailed plan 277

Don't Assume 277

Prepare the Scope of Work 278

Make Sure You Are All in Agreement 279

Dealing with Service Providers 280

Do Not Alter Your Decisions 281

Have a Contingency in Place 282

Don't Pay Contractors for Work Before
Completion 282
Ensure You Are Physically Present.....................283
Know Your Suppliers..284
Hire an Expert...285

Chapter 13: Agent Versus FSBO *286*

Is it Compulsory to Hire Real Estate Agents? 286

**FSBO or For Sale by Owner: What Does it
Mean?... 287**
Agent vs. FSBO: Fees 287
Marketing 288
Time..288
Negotiation 289
Legal Assistance 290

Which Is the Ideal Option For You? 290

Chapter 14: Staging *291*

Staging A Home: What Does it Mean? 291

Does Staging Work? 292
Use Neutral Colors 292
Clean and Clean Some More 293

Keep Things Fresh 293
Let There Be Light...294
First Stage the Vital Rooms 295
Rent Some Furniture 295
Don't Ignore the Curb 296

Chapter 15: The Closing Process *298*

What Is a Closing? 298

House Closing Process for Sellers 299

Negotiating 299

Closing Costs 300

Agent Percentage 301

Buyer's Due Diligence 301

Closing 302

When Is Your Property Categorized as Sold? . 303

Conclusion *304*

Rental Property Investing

Complete Beginner's Guide on How to Create Wealth, Passive Income and Financial Freedom with Apartments and Multifamily Real Estate Investing Even with No Money Down

Introduction

Are you interested in increasing your wealth by investing in rental properties, but you aren't certain where to begin? Do you think that rental property investing is a good idea for you? Do you want to invest without having to worry about any expensive mortgages or down payments? If yes, then this is the perfect book for you. This book is a beginner's guide to learning about rental property investing. If you are a first-time investor, then I am quite certain that you have plenty of questions. Well, in today's tech-dominated world, a simple Google search can provide you with plenty of information. However, the wealth of information available online can be quite scary, especially for a beginner. That's where this book comes in. Don't worry, because this book will become your go-to guide to learning about rental property investing.

In this book, you will learn everything there is to know about rental property investing. You will learn if rental property investing is a good option for you, the steps to buying your first property, different things you must consider while buying a rental property, how to analyze the property, raising funds to buy your first rental property, how to manage the property, and much more. Rental property investing is a great way to generate additional income or even passive income. Regardless of your reason for investing, you must understand all the different aspects involved in investing if you want to be profitable.

So, if you are ready to step into the world of rental property investing, let us get started without further ado!

Chapter 1: Rental Property

101

Rental property investing is a great idea - however, how can you determine whether it is the right idea for you or not? As with any other form of investment, there are certain pros and cons involved in rental properties. To begin with, let's talk about the benefits and the possible drawbacks of rental property investing.

Pros and Cons of Rental Property Investing

Direct income

The most obvious benefit of investing in rental properties is that you will be receiving income from your renters. It is a direct source of income. The monthly checks you receive will go directly to your monthly income. For instance, if you decide to rent a property for about $1000 a month, that's $12,000 in the form of additional income per year. Even if this number sounds rather optimistic to you, you stand to gain at least 75% of this from rents. It certainly is a good source of additional income. Apart from this, it is a great source of passive income. Once you rent your property, you don't have to do anything other than collect rents and ensure the property is well maintained. You don't have to quit your day job to become a rental property investor. If you want to, you can always hire a property manager to take care of the property. By doing this, you can drastically reduce the efforts involved in managing the property and can collect your rent checks with no hassle on your end.

Appreciation of the property

Since you happen to own the property, you will stand to gain when the property's value appreciates. Over time, the value of the property does appreciate. So, if you do want to sell in the future, you can expect a profit from the sale.

Sweat equity

Whenever you upgrade the property or make any improvements to it, it increases the sweat equity of the property. If you repaint, get some landscaping done or refurbish it, the property's value will increase. Whenever the value of the property increases, the rent you can demand for the property increases, too. All of this means that it will increase your income.

Tax benefits

There are a couple of tax deductions you can claim as a property owner. All the deductions will help reduce your taxes and increase your earnings. For instance, one of the most considerable deductions available to the owner of a rental property is the interest paid toward the mortgage or any other loan. Any interest payable on a loan that is taken to acquire or improve the property is a deductible expense. The deduction of real estate depreciation is another tax concession available. Also, the cost of any ordinary and necessary repairs of a reasonable amount is deductible, too, like the costs incurred to fix the floor, gutters or any leaks, replacement of a broken window, and more. If you decide to use any of your personal property to further a rental activity, then such property is applicable to tax deductions. Any insurance premiums you pay for the rental property along with any professional or legal services you hire for the maintenance of the rental property are eligible for tax concessions. All in all, these deductions help reduce your tax liability.

As with any other investment, there are certain drawbacks of investing in a rental property, and they are as follows.

If you decide to invest in a rental property, then you must be prepared to allocate a significant share of your assets toward this investment. At least, that's is the case for an average investor. The problem crops up when there is no diversification of your assets. All investors hope to gain profits from their potential investments. However, if it doesn't go as planned and the returns you earn aren't favorable, then you can incur a loss. But don't you fret, because in this book you will learn about different things you can do to ensure your rental property proves to be a profitable investment.

Finding a good tenant is quite important. If you end up with a troublesome tenant, you might find yourself in a sticky situation. What will you do if the tenant doesn't pay rent on time or damages the property? Finding a good tenant is quintessential.

Once you rent out a property, your work doesn't end there. You don't have to be involved in maintaining the property at all times, but you do need to show some involvement. No stream of income is 100% passive, and the same stands true for rental property investing, too. There are certain expenses you need to cover while renting out a property. You can certainly deduct some expenses, but there are limits established for every deductible expense, and anything above that limit is payable by you.

So, there are certain drawbacks, but when it comes to rental property investing, the benefits it offers easily outweigh the drawbacks. A little effort and due diligence can help overcome those drawbacks, too.

Identify Your Investment Goals

Now that you are aware of all the different benefits you stand to gain from investing in rental property, you must identify your investment goals. Why do you want to invest? Failure to plan is translated into planning to fail. It is quintessential to have a sense of purpose, regardless of what you want to do. So, what's the purpose of investing? The reasons for investing will vary from one person to another. Without a plan, it is unlikely that the odds will be in your favor. Without a goal and a plan to achieve that goal, the investment you plan to make will not do you much good. Why do you need a goal? A goal helps motivate you even when obstacles crop up. Only when you consider your goal will you be able to estimate your budget and the associated risks and returns you want.

So, before you can start investing, it is time to think about your investment goals. Do you wish to save for your retirement? Do you want to create a fund for a rainy day? Do you want to create an additional source of income? Does the idea of passive income appeal to you? Do you want to save for your child's education or some other reason? The reasons for investing are quite varied, and you must understand your motivation to invest.

Take some time and think about the different reasons you want to invest. Once you are aware of the reasons, it is time to classify them. Categorize your goals as short-term and long-term goals. A short-term goal might be to save for an exotic vacation, whereas a long-term goal would be to save for your retirement and so on. You get the idea, right? Don't make a mental list of your goals. Instead, make a physical note of the goals. It is always a good idea to write them down. When you make a list of your goals and glance at it regularly, it will act as a motivating factor.

Once you are aware of your goals, you need to make them money specific. The goal "I want to save for an exotic vacation" is quite vague. It neither includes a time limit nor a monetary value. So, the next step is to attach a monetary value to your goals. For instance, if you want to save for a trip to Italy for a week, you need around $15,000 for it. Try to set a monetary value so that you know how much you need to earn to attain that goal.

Principles of Success

Who doesn't desire or dream about success? Everyone does, but only a few tend to be successful. Did you ever wonder why this happens? If real estate investing is profitable, then why aren't all real estate investors successful? Well, there are certain habits that all successful people share. In this section, you will learn about the five principles for succeeding as a rental property investor.

Learn to manage efficiently

Regardless of whether you are a newbie or a veteran investor, the first key element of becoming a successful rental property investor is to become a good manager. You might have a property manager, or you might want to self-manage, but regardless of which you choose, you still need to be a good manager. Being an owner of rental property is like learning to walk a tightrope. You need to keep moving on that narrow line, and even when a gust of wind threatens to blow you over, you must maintain your balance and keep going. The metaphorical "gust of wind" in the world of rental property investing can come in different forms. It can be in the form of natural disasters, untrustworthy property managers, bad tenants, poor economic conditions, and so on. These things can easily make you falter if you aren't careful. Don't assume that by merely purchasing a property and renting it out, your work ends. Apart from managing the properties, you need to manage your finances. Ensure that you are keeping track of all your expenses in an orderly fashion along with the income you are earning if you want to become a successful investor.

Increasing your income

As you make your way through investing, one of your goals must be to increase your income from rental properties. I am not implying that you need to keep increasing the rent, even if it is an important means of increasing your rental income. You must ensure that the property you rent is never less than the market rate. Now, you might be thinking that renting the property at a price less than the market rate might spell less drama. It might be true, but what is the opportunity cost involved?

Please keep in mind that becoming a rental property investor is like starting a business. Profit needs to be one of your goals if you want to be successful. The more rental units you own, the more problematic it becomes if you rent them out below the market rate. For instance, if you have five units and you rent them out at $100 less than the market rate, then you stand to lose $500 per month and $6000 per year. Now, I am not saying that you need to price the property too high. If you over or under price the rent of the property, then you stand to lose and not gain.

If you want to invest in a property, you must be aware of all the numbers involved. This means it is time to crunch some numbers. You must do the necessary research about the prevailing market rate in the immediate locality. You must also be aware of all the expenses involved.

Reduce the expenses

You will need to work on reducing your expenses. You don't have to become a miserly landlord, but you need to cut costs while making sure that your tenants stay happy. For instance, you can opt for energy-saving appliances in the rental unit. You can transfer the payment of utility bills like water, garbage, and electricity over to the tenant. Compare the insurance policies available to get the best possible rates and the like. These are simple ways in which you can reduce the expenses involved. At times, even a small change can help improve your bottom line.

The property matters

The location of the property is one of the most important aspects of rental property investing. For instance, if you decide to invest in a rental property that is located in an area with poor connectivity, then it is unlikely that you will find a tenant and even if you do, they might not agree to pay a high rent. The location of the property dictates the amount you can quote as rent. Likewise, if you decide to invest in an extremely noisy and polluted industrial area, the demand for the property might not be too high.

Tenants

It isn't merely about finding an ideal property to invest in; you must also find suitable tenants. You must screen all potential tenants while renting out a property. Regardless of how wonderful the property is, without the right tenants, you will not profit. You must ensure you are aware of who your tenants are, their rental record, as well as obtain any past references or records that provide details about them. You must also perform a background check to ensure the potential tenants can pay the rent.

Investing Strategies

Well, you have a rented property, and you might have a few questions. What's next? What is your exit strategy? How can you make money? Some real estate investors buy rental property to repair and then turn it over. Some tend to buy them and hold onto them so they have an excellent source of passive income, while others buy them to sell them later when they need money. Which is the best way? Well, the answer is that there isn't a perfect answer to this question. The key is to know the type of investor you want to be. Here are some options that you can consider.

If you want to hold onto the property for five years or less, you have to flip it. In the early 2000s, house flipping was all the rage. House flipping is still a good strategy today. It requires more patience. Usually, a flipper will purchase the real estate, upgrade it, and then sell it after a couple of months. This investment strategy usually appeals to a conservative or a part-time investor who likes the idea of flipping and tends to have a five-year plan ready. They usually like to take things slowly and then make improvements to the property, rent it out, and then finally sell the property when the market is ripe.

You do not have to sell rentals, even if the real estate market is currently hot. As long as you have stable cash flow, you do not have to sell the property, and this can be a good source of passive income for you. You can keep writing off depreciation on the property for tax purposes until you reach a certain limit. Investors tend to hold onto the property until they can write off the depreciation, and when they cannot, they sell the property.

The third strategy is to keep the property and know that you will sell it when an event occurs that causes a sale. You may plan to sell the property when your child is in college, or for other expenses that you know will be incurred in the future. Some people manage to sell real estate before major repairs such as a new roof are required. However, you may have to sell it at a lower price if you sell a home that requires major repairs. You can, however, use it in the meantime by borrowing it.

If you lose money on a property, you probably want to get rid of it by selling it. Maybe the market has changed and you cannot rent it, maybe insurance or even taxes have soared and you cannot make a profit if you can sell it. There are many things that you need to consider to weigh variables such as the losses that you might incur each month and the scope of any favorable changes before you decide to get rid of the property.

As you have noticed, there is no right answer to this question. Nobody can tell you how long you have to keep the rental property. If you have a plan, stick to it and do not be deterred by market fluctuations.

Type of Investment

If you now want to buy a rental property, you have to choose the type of property you want to buy. There are three main types of real estate to choose from, and they are single-units, multi-unit residential units, and commercial properties.

Single-family units

The best option for an investor who has never rented property before is a single residential property. They are often cheaper and do not require much maintenance compared to other options. You can invest easily in a single-family unit. It has no common walls, and it is built in a plot by itself. They usually have a front or back yard. Since you are the owner, you are responsible for all maintenance costs incurred on the unit. They tend to attract long-term tenants who are financially sustainable. The resale value of such units is also quite high. The next option is to buy an apartment or a condominium. These are individual units which are part of a large complex or community with common walls. It offers a variety of amenities, including a gym, a club, and a pool. Since you are the owner of the apartment, you are part of a homeowner or a condominium community and have to pay a monthly fee. Maintenance costs are low compared to residential properties consisting of single units. The third option is a townhouse. A townhouse is a mix of a single-family home and an apartment. They usually have common walls with adjoining houses in the neighborhood.

Multi-residential units

These usually consist of two to six portions or units, which an investor buys as a form of investment. A typical situation is when the owner owns the entire building. The owner can live in an apartment and rent the remaining units. The maintenance costs incurred are slightly higher when compared to other forms of real estate investment. However, since they consist of multiple units, the potential for generating higher cash flow is possible.

Real Estate Investment Team

Real estate agents

Everyone wants to make smart decisions whenever there is an economic strain. While investing in a rental property, every penny you spend counts. Everyone has specific criterion when buying a home. Some people want a large house with a pool, and some prefer a cozy apartment. If you are looking for something specific, it is better to seek advice from a professional real estate agent before investing in real estate. You know the exact features that fit your budget and needs, and they can help you with the documentation and throughout the transactional process. A real estate agent will also keep you informed about any other potential properties you can invest in. Some of the benefits of consulting a real estate agent are as follows:

Real estate agents have the right knowledge about making a good deal. They know the right procedures and formalities required to buy and sell real estate. They can also give you the information you need and suggest the right properties, depending on your needs. They also know about the local, state, national, and international market, so they can help you select the ideal property. All of this is possible only if you opt for a good and knowledgeable real estate agent.

Real estate agents who have been in the market for a long time have reliable contacts - people who can provide them the necessary information. By hiring the services of the real estate agent, it also gives you access to such contacts. Apart from this, it also gives you the chance to develop a better connection in the local market and be aware of the properties that you can buy, sell, or rent. They can also enable you to make a profitable decision for your business. They have professional partnerships and contacts in the market and can provide you with a compiled list of contacts they have worked with before.

We all know how cumbersome documentation work is when a property needs to be sold or bought. Real estate agents have gone through this process many times and can help you avoid paperwork mistakes, saving you time and money in the future. Real estate agents will help you to effectively negotiate prices and terms with the other party on your behalf. This will save you trouble and unnecessary tension. These brokers have exceptional negotiation skills. Real estate agents are very experienced and know the value of the land or property and can be sure that you will pay the right price. They can help you find the perfect solution for your budget.

Property manager

There are certain things that you need to consider while deciding whether you want to use the services of a property manager or not. To determine this, you can create a list that things that you need to do, what you cannot do, along with the tasks you don't want to undertake. By hiring a property manager, you no longer have to deal with the tenant's complaints.

Who doesn't like the idea of earning passive income from renting real estate? However, this also means that you have to deal with all the problems and complaints of the tenants. If you use the services of a property manager, you do not have to worry about it. A real estate manager does all of this for you. Your real estate manager will be responsible for things like the selection of tenants. Your real estate manager will take care of all the time-consuming aspects of finding the right tenants for your property. You don't have to spend your precious time checking up on your rental property. For example, the property manager takes care of checking the tenants, site visits, evictions, and so on.

Take a look at the successful real estate magnates, who have managed to accumulate enormous wealth. Do you think they did it all by themselves? Of course, they would not have been able to achieve all their success if they had personally answered every complaint lodged by the renter or had personally corrected the plumbing work on the individual units. They are successful because they are good at prioritizing the tasks and know what is important and what isn't. By hiring a property manager, you can focus your attention on the important aspects of being a landlord.

A real estate management firm offers all kinds of professional services you may need to maintain your property, and you don't have to worry about solving the problem yourself. You save time, energy, and money. You can also do more and sleep better at night, knowing that your investments are in safe hands. Most real estate investors tend to have certain voluntary restrictions on investing in other markets. This is not necessarily bad, but you should not hold back your business. If you have a good property manager, there is no reason why you should not live in another city if you want. You don't have to go to inspect the property physically. The property manager does it all for you. However, I do suggest that it is wise to supervise the work done by the property manager constantly.

A good real estate manager always has your best interests in mind. Before investing in real estate, you can consult with your real estate manager to see if this is a good investment or not. You can ask them various questions about the area you are interested in, the percentage of vacancies, the trends in the local market, the expected rent for real estate, the cost of buying real estate, examining potential real estate and so on. Your real estate manager is your personal advisor who will help you make the best investment decisions.

Hiring a real estate manager is a really good idea. The services they provide outweigh the cost of their hiring. Be careful when you hire a property manager, as the responsibility for the care of your property lies with them. You want someone who can look after your investments and develop them further. You can also focus on other things that require your attention. You can enjoy a steady stream of passive income without having to worry about the various issues involved in maintaining various projects. If you have a few investments in real estate, a real estate manager will help you a lot.

Chapter 2: Sample Plans

Develop a Business Plan

A wish becomes a goal when it is supported with a plan. If you want to get into the business of rental property investing, then you need a business plan to make your dream more realistic. Why do you need a business plan? Well, it helps create a system and set benchmarks to help you successfully create a stream of passive income. Are you wondering what a business plan looks like? In this section, you will learn about the different steps you must follow to create a rental property business plan.

Before getting started, you must understand what a rental property business means. It refers to a venture wherein an investor purchases and manages one or more properties intending to earn a steady income. These properties can be in the form of single or multiple units, which are rented out in exchange for monthly rent. Getting started with rental property investing is like starting any other business. You must figure out the different financing options, do the necessary research, gather the resources, network, and identify your target audience.

So, are you an owner of a rental property business? Well, renting a house can be considered to be a business. This is quite a controversial topic, and there are two ways to look at it. From the perspective of finance, renting a residential property is a source of passive income. Investors aren't liable to pay self-employment tax when it comes to the income derived from rental property or properties. In this sense, renting out properties is not considered to be a business in the strict sense of the word according to tax liabilities. However, from the standpoint of a career option, a lot of people tend to make a full-time income from this passive source. Renting properties can be considered to be a full-fledged business when you think about it from this perspective.

Here are all the steps you must follow for writing a rental property business plan.

- Setting your goals to earn a passive income.

- Selecting the ideal rental property market.

- Estimating all your expenses and the sources of finance.

- Developing a marketing strategy.

- Managing the rental property by yourself

or seek outside help.

Let us look at these steps in detail now.

Step one: Setting your passive income goals

Finding tenants is an important part of rental property investing, but it isn't restricted to just that. It is about setting certain goals for this venture, like the time and energy you can direct toward this passive income opportunity. There are two questions you must answer to establish your passive income goals.

How much time and money can you invest? How much passive income do you wish to earn per month?

Step two: Selecting your market

Selecting your market is almost as important as the amount of capital you are willing to invest or the experience you want to gain. There are different factors which influence this decision. However, here are a couple of questions you can use to determine your ideal market.

- Do you want to invest in a distant market?

- If yes, then how distant a market can you invest in?

- Do you have a team to help you handle the daily affairs, or are you willing to commute?

- What is the average rental rate in the market?

- What is the average market price of the property?

You don't necessarily have to live in the vicinity of the market you wish to invest in. That said, this doesn't mean you don't have to understand the market. Once you answer these questions, you will have an ideal market in your mind.

Step three: Estimating all your expenses and the sources of finance

A major hurdle every rental property investor must overcome is figuring out the finances. If you have an estimate of all the different expenses you stand to incur for acquiring and maintaining the rental property, it will give you some much-needed clarity. Your business plan must answer the following questions:

- How much capital will you need to get started?

- How do you plan on raising the capital you need if you don't have it?

- What will be the cost of repairs involved?

- Are there any recurring monthly expenses you will incur? If yes, then what are the expenses?

After you do this, you must also make the offer.

You like the property you want to buy. What do you do next? The next step is to submit the offer for the property.

The process of making an offer to buy a property may vary from state to state. In some areas, verbal communication is appropriate; in others, written consent is required. For various legal reasons, it is advisable to make a written agreement. It helps to get rid of all the confusion and worries. If you have legal problems, you are safe. Negotiations begin when you meet with an agent. The agent will ask you questions to assess your situation and understand what type of property you need. There will be many phone calls, negotiations, and reviews before you can make an offer.

Make sure you fully understand the bidding process. Ask the agent to explain how this process works and contact your lawyer. It is a good idea to consult a financial adviser before deciding on an investment. Know the price you are willing to pay for the property (maximum and minimum restrictions). Remember that this is a negotiation, so be prepared for some back and forth. Research the property extensively. The property should be at your discretion, and in the end, you will invest a significant portion of your finances. Remember the sales motivation of the seller, the date of the calculation, and all the other information you need. You have to be patient, as this is not a process that you can complete overnight. Some property purchases take longer than others. You can ask your lawyer to sign a contract of sale. If the seller suggests the same thing, make sure your lawyer approves it before deciding to sign anything. After all the documents are in order, you can contact your financier to get the allocation approval.

Step four: Marketing strategies

The first step to creating passive income is to purchase a rental property. After that, at some point, you must make a plan about how you can attract tenants to your property. Having a wonderful property that is fully furnished and equipped will do you no good if your target audience isn't aware of it. So, you need to make a list of ways in which you can reach your potential tenants. The most commonly used strategies include publishing ads on rental websites and social networking sites, in print media, by word of mouth through local realtors, local bulletin boards, and the old-school means of word of mouth publicity.

The marketing channel you opt for will depend on your target market. The more specific your marketing strategies are, the easier it will be for you to plan your marketing expenses.

Step five: Managing the rental property

Managing the rental property is quintessential. It involves the managing of all the different systems you must establish to keep the property in good condition and to keep the cash flow going. It doesn't mean you can hire a property manager and leave it all to them. Even if you hire a property manager, you will still need to supervise them. Here are some questions you must answer to understand how you want to manage the property.

- Do you want to be the landlord and self-manage, or do you want to hire a property manager?

- Who will be responsible for finding and screening the tenants?

- Who will look after the upkeep and maintenance of the property?

- Who will look after the basic maintenance of the property like yard maintenance?

The answers to these questions will essentially depend on your budget and the time you wish to allocate. Once you go through all these steps, you will have a clear business plan in mind for rental property investing. Once you have a plan ready, it becomes quite easy to manage the property and avoid any last-minute surprises.

Chapter 3: How to Find Rental Properties

Different Sources to Consider

There are several ways in which potential investors can find rental properties available for sale. When you use multiple sources, you give yourself a chance to find the best properties to invest in. Here are a couple of ways in which you can find great properties.

Through your network

Finding rental properties through networking is a good idea since it helps you discover properties that people might not usually be aware of. Since not a lot of people know about such properties, you might be able to get a good deal on those properties. There are three ways in which you can find properties via networking, and these are through a personal investor network, through any personal acquaintances, and investment clubs.

A personal investor network refers to the database of investors you might have been collecting over months or years that you have been an investor, or it is the database you must start maintaining from now on. It can include the contacts of other landlords you met who own rental properties in the same area as you or anyone else who is an investor and you are well-versed with. Investment clubs are a great way to create useful contacts because they often have an email list wherein members tend to share and advertise real estate properties. If you aren't a member of an investment club, then it is a good idea to become a member now. Most real estate investment clubs tend to charge an annual membership fee of around $100 to $300. Think of this fee as an investment because you stand a chance to gain a lot of valuable information. Your personal network of acquaintances is a great place to start, too. You must remember that those involved in real estate aren't the only ones who can give you access to good investments. Your personal network can include your friends, family members, colleagues, lawyers, accountants, or anyone else along these lines, and they can be great sources of help while you're searching for investment properties. Those who are a part of your personal network might have come across, seen, or heard about some properties that might interest you. Also, if you know any contractors, even they can be an ideal source to network with other landlords or investors.

Find properties online

There are various websites you can use to search for any potential rental property investments. These sites usually offer several resources ranging from a general sale to more refined searches like short sales or foreclosure properties. Some websites even offer information about neighborhoods along with property records that you can analyze to gauge whether the property is a good investment or not.

Realtors can be helpful

There are a couple of different ways in which you can use realtors while searching for rental properties. For instance, if you come across any interesting listings, you can always contact the realtor to arrange a viewing of the property, or you can even view the listings online on their websites. You can contact real estate offices or other realtors who work in the areas you are interested in and inquire about any potential investment properties. You can also enlist the help of a realtor to help you search for potential properties. Realtors tend to have lists of all available properties or have contacts, which might help you.

Don't overlook the print media

You can always find local listings in print media. It might sound a little old-fashioned, but this approach works, too. Some of the properties advertised in print media might not be listed online, so the competition for such properties isn't too high. One of the best sources to find local listings is the newspaper. You can find several "for sale by owner" properties along with properties listed by realtors in your local newspaper. Apart from this, you can also search for rental properties in any local marketing publications. You can find such publications in your local grocery stores and such.

Auctions

Property auctions are also a great way to find good real estate deals. There are different types of auctions you can attend, like online auctions, private auctions, and sheriff sale auctions. A quick Google search can help you find any online auctions for properties in the areas you are interested in. You can also use a site like auction.com to find online auctions. A sheriff sale auction will usually be held in the county's town hall, courthouse, or even the sheriff's office. Usually, foreclosed properties are sold to the public in these auctions. If a specific foreclosed property has not been sold, then the same will be listed as an REO or real estate owned with a local real estate agent. The final option is to look at private auctions held by companies. These auctions are usually contracted by lenders for selling multiple properties at once.

Steps for Choosing an Investment Property

If you have been considered investing in a real estate property, then there are certain steps you must follow while choosing the right property to maximize your investment.

The first thing you must do is talk to others. This means you must first get a feel of the market you want to invest in by talking to other real estate investors in that area. You can attend a meeting of any real estate association in the immediate vicinity to understand the market. Not just that, but as mentioned earlier, networking is one of the best ways to find real estate properties for investing in.

Once you do this, you must estimate all the costs you will acquire in the process of investing in a rental property. It is seldom that an average individual has all the necessary capital just lying around. So, if you want to invest, you must get your finances in order and determine the capital you will need to borrow. Before you start getting excited about any listing, you must also be aware of the costs involved. It is better to prepare in advance to avoid any unpleasant surprises like a monthly payment that's higher than what you imagined.

Now, you must take some time and think about who you want to rent the property to and the kind of neighborhood that will appeal to such tenants. You must find a property that easily fits in with the rest of the neighborhood. For instance, it is not a good idea to invest all your hard-earned money into a tiny dingy studio located in a suburban neighborhood. It is certainly easier to find tenants if you invest in a property that's appropriate for your chosen market.

The TV series Fixer Upper is certainly interesting, but I suggest that a newbie investor steer clear of all fixer-uppers. It is okay to work on improving the appearance of the property like fixing the tiles, repainting the house and such, but you must steer clear of all such works that are related to the core structure of the house like electrical and piping works. If the property you are looking for is absolutely perfect, but the monthly payments related to it are quite high, then I suggest you try house hacking. House hacking refers to the practice of residing in the property for at least a year (when you purchase a duplex and live in one portion or buy a single-family home and rent it to roommates), and it helps you earn a little while making the necessary payments. Not just that, it also becomes quite easy to manage and maintain the property.

Once you find a potential property to invest in, you must acquire all the information related to it. The first step is to figure out the income you stand to gain through rents. If the property was previously let out, then you can ask the previous owner about the property's rental history and compare the rates to those of other properties. A quick online search can also help you understand the current rental rates in the area. If not, you can check in with a local real estate office to get a better idea.

Now, you must tally all your expenses. While estimating your expenses, it is always better to overstate the expenses. So, if the rent you can expect per month is $2000, then you can set $1000 toward different expenses you can expect per month. If you need to pay an EMI of $800 per month, then you can expect a cash flow of $200 from the property. There are different expenses you must consider while making these calculations. You need to include the charges for essential utilities like garbage or water, maintenance costs, major expenses in the form of any repairs, fee of the local homeowners association (if there is one), at least set one month's rent aside for a potential "vacancy," and taxes or insurance. You will learn more about calculating the total cash flow from the property in the following chapters.

Appreciation of the rental property

There are two types of appreciation in the property's value, and they are forced and market appreciation. If you purchase a property and make any repairs, then you are essentially increasing the value of the place, and this is known as forced appreciation. If the neighborhood the property is located in improves over time, then the value of the property is bound to increase, too, and this is known as market appreciation. A new investor must not focus on forced appreciation, because it can be difficult to make a cost-benefit analysis of all the repairs.

On the other hand, market appreciation is easier to estimate, and you can do this by using historical market appreciation data. However, please don't purchase a property only because you think its value will appreciate in the future. A new investor must look for properties that will help generate income, regardless of their value of appreciation, and this is exactly what I suggest you do.

Return rate

There are a couple more calculations you are required to perform. You must estimate your cash on cash rate. For instance, if you invested $100,000 purchasing the property, and if you stand to gain $12,000 per year, then the cash on cash return rate is 12%. A good cash-on-cash return is any number that's over 10%. Before you make a purchase, I suggest you analyze at least two dozen property deals to figure out the cash on cash return rate. However, this must not be the only criterion you use to make a purchase. Also check the condition of the property.

Calculate the capitalization rate

The capitalization, or cap rate, is the time it will take to recover your initial investment. If your initial investment was $100,000 and you earn $5000 annually after deducting all expenses, then the cap rate is 5%. This means it will take you 20 years to recover your investment. If your earnings from the property are $10,000 per year, then the cap rate is 10%, and you will take ten years to recover the initial investment. You will learn more about using the cap rate to analyze a property in the following chapters.

1% Rule

As a rule of thumb, I suggest you use the one percent rule while evaluating any rental properties. If the rent you receive before any expenses is at least 1% of the total purchase price, then the property is a good investment. For instance, if you are purchasing a property for $100,000, then the rent you can expect from it must at least be $1000.

Chapter 4: Analyzing a Rental Property

Unlike a stock market investment, ascertaining the exact value of a property you own or wish to purchase is slightly tricky. In this chapter, you will learn about different aspects you must consider while analyzing a rental property's value.

The Big Picture

When you are trying to analyze the value of a property, you must consider certain essential aspects like the ones discussed in this section.

Income matters

When you are investing in rental property, you must be able to ascertain the realistic income you stand to gain from the property and whether it will be sustainable for you. The present and historical data about the rents related to the property matter. Once you are aware of the income range, then you will be able to calculate the gross earnings from the property and compare this against the numbers of other properties in the same area.

Price appreciation

A housing bubble takes place, and then a crash soon follows. This phenomenon occurs because investors tend to forget about the income component of the property and instead solely focus on the property's potential for appreciation. This was the main reason for the most well-known real estate crash. Investors were not interested in the negative cash flow they had to endure and instead concentrated only on the profits they could gain from a flip within a year or two. Once the party came to a standstill, speculators were crushed and this, in turn, caused a domino effect which hurt all those who were in the "buy and hold" stage of the property. If your primary focus is on the appreciation of the property's value in the future instead of the income, then you are a speculator. Real estate holds no true value until it can generate income for the owner.

Property price and inflation

A property's price will appreciate only if the inflation is around +/- 2%. Simply put, if the current rate of inflation is around 3%, then you can expect a national increase in property prices by 1-5%. Over time, the price can fluctuate drastically. However, if you observe the prices of property for over ten years, you will be able to see an obvious correlation. If you have an impression that the prices of property will increase at a steady rate of 10% per year, then I hate to break your bubble. You must only think of the property's appreciation as a secondary factor and not a primary attribute. If the value does increase, it is amazing. If not, then you will at least have cash flowing in.

Property is localized

Don't place too much emphasis on national property statistics. Just because the prices of property are going up in one region doesn't mean the same statistics apply to you as well. Forget about national statistics while analyzing the property's value. Instead, you must stick to local market trends.

Specific Steps to Follow

Calculate the annual gross yield

Consider the realistic existing monthly rate of rent in the market according to comparables and multiply it by 12 to get your gross annual yield from the property. Now, you must divide the gross yield you get by the current market price of the property. For instance, let us assume the market price of the property is $500,000. If the rent is $2000 per month, it gives you $24,000 per year. Now, divide $24,000 by $500,000. It gives you a gross yield of 4.8%. The annual gross yield is a quick way to analyze what you stand to gain from the property given that you are acquiring the property without a loan and don't have any other ongoing expenditures.

Compare the gross rental yield to the risk-free rate

The risk-free rate is defined as the yield of a 10-year US bond. Investors term it as risk-free because it is practically impossible that the US government will default on any of their debt payments. All investment decisions you make require a risk premium that's more than the risk-free rate. Or else, you must ask yourself why you are even risking all your hard-earned money. If the annual gross rental yield of the property is less than the risk-free rate, then you must either negotiate a better deal or search for another property.

Calculate the annual net rent yield

The net rent yield is essentially your net operating income from the property divided by the market value of the property. It is quite easy to calculate the net annual income. You must subtract the expenses like interest on the mortgage, insurance premiums, property taxes, marketing, and maintenance cost of the property and HOA dues from the gross annual income of the property. Simply put, you must calculate the profit you stand to earn.

For instance, let's say the annual rent is $24,000, the HOA dues are $3000, property taxes amount to $4800, the insurance costs $500, the maintenance is about $1000, and the mortgage interest is $10000. This means your total expenses account for $19,700, and your net income from the property is $4300. So, to calculate the net rental yield, you must divide $4300/$500,000. The net rental yield in this situation is 1%. As long as the cash flow from the rental property stays positive, all is well. However, the margin can differ from one person to another.

Compare the net rental yield to the risk-free rate

The net rental yield must at least be equal to or higher than the risk-free rate. You will repay the initial principal over time, and it will increase the net rental yield and spread over the risk-free rate. If all goes as it should, then the rents will increase along with your property's value.

Price to earnings ratio

The price to earnings ratio is the market value of the property divided by the net operating profits from the property. In the above example, the price to earnings ratio is 106 (i.e., $500,000/$4700). So, that means the investor needs 106 years of net profits to make back the initial investment. This doesn't sound too good, but it is only an example. In this example, it is assumed that the owner never pays down the mortgage, and the rent stays constant - both of these situations are highly unlikely. A better way to crunch numbers is to divide the market price of the property by the gross rental income. In the above example, when you follow this formula, it gives you 20.8. It essentially means it will take the property 20.8 years to pay for itself. The lower the price to earnings ratio, the better deal it is.

Property price and rental expectations forecast

The price to earnings ratio along with the rental yield rate are ways to check the income the property will generate, provided everything works favorably. Apart from ratios, you must also concentrate on several external factors while determining whether a specific property is a good investment or not. The best way to forecast what the future holds in store for you is to compare what happened in the past and past real estate development and establish realistic expectations about certain external factors. The external factors that I am referring to are the local employment growth, city permits for development, tax respites, and such. When all these factors are favorable, then the rental price, as well as the value of the property, will increase.

Various situations

Now, you need to establish a realistic property price

along with rental forecasts for various scenarios. For instance, if the rental value decreases for the next five years at a rate of 5% per year, will you be able to handle this decrease? If the mortgage rates increase from 3.5% to 5%, how will this influence the demand for real estate? You must be prepared to deal with things if they don't go as you planned. You must develop certain exit strategies to leave the market when things become unfavorable. You will learn more about exit strategies in the following chapters.

Taxes and depreciation

Most of the expenses you incur while maintaining and owning a rental property offer tax deductions, including the interest payable on the mortgage as well as property taxes. Depreciation is a non-cash item that not only decreases your Net Operating Income, but it also reduces your taxes. If you reside in the property for at least two years out of the past five years, then $250,000 and $500,000 of profits are considered to be tax-free for individuals and married couples respectively. There is also a tax provision, the 1031 exchange, which allows an investor to sell a specific property, then reinvest all the proceeds from the sale into a new property while deferring all capital gains taxes.

Cash Flow Analysis

Cash flow refers to the income you are left with from a specific business after you clear all your dues and pay all the necessary bills. In the business of rental property investing, cash flow represents the income you are left with in hand after you pay for different expenses like mortgage, insurance, vacancies, capital expenditure, taxes, utilities, and any other property-related expenses. Cash flow is one of the basic things you need to calculate, and it is quite easy to calculate.

Cash flow = Total income – Total expenditure

It is as simple as that, but a lot of people get it wrong because there are several items you must consider while calculating. If you miss out on even one item, it will affect your cash flow.

Total income

The total income is often the same as the total rent you earn, although at times it might not be. There are a couple of sources of income you must include like application fees, laundry income, and late fees. While analyzing the cash flow from a property, it is a good idea to make a list of all the possible sources of income. While estimating the income you stand to earn, opt for a conservative approach. Essentially, it is a good accounting practice, especially while making estimates, to understate the income and overstate the expenses you might incur. It is a better idea to err on the side of caution and assume you might not get as much as you are hoping to get.

Total expenses

This is the aspect of calculating the slightly tricky cash flow. Most people are good at estimating their income, but when it comes to expenses, making even one mistake can spell the difference between success and failure. While you are dealing with rental properties, there are several expenses you will incur. For instance, here are all the expenses you might incur, just off the top of my head:

The mortgage, property taxes, mortgage insurance, flood insurance, property hazard insurance, earthquake insurance, sewer, garbage, water, repairs, propane, natural gas, electricity, general maintenance, new appliances, landscaping, capital expenditure, software, gas or mileage, office supplies, Homeowners Association dues and fees, city taxes, payroll, property management costs, vacancy rate, advertising, marketing, and a couple of other expenses I might have overlooked.

Apart from making a list of all possible expenses, you must understand that each of these expenses might not be monthly. So, it is a good idea to calculate the specific percentage of those expenses while planning. For instance, your rental property unit might not be vacant right now, but you must function under the assumption that it might be empty at least one month per year. Therefore, while calculating your total expenses, you might want to include vacancy expense as 1/12th of the annual rent. Various expenses like your office supplies or even gas can be ignored while dealing with a single house, but you must consider them if you are dealing with a multi-family rental unit.

Here is an example of how to calculate cash flow to help you understand what each of these items translates into:

Let us take the example of Homer, who is trying to calculate his monthly cash flow from a two-unit family house he wants to buy. According to the local real estate agent, Homer can rent out this property for $600 per unit. He will need to pay $50 for garbage and $125 for water or sewer per month. The real estate agent informs him that the properties like the one he wants to buy tend to stay vacant for 5% of the year. Homer estimates that he will need to spend around 8% per month on all the repairs. Apart from this, he plans on keeping 5% aside every month toward capital expenditures like installation of a new roof, a new heating system, or any other major property-related expenses. Homer has a mortgage on the popery, and his mortgage payment will be around $470 per month without taxes or insurance. The yearly property taxes amount to $960 per year, and the insurance is about $600 per year. Finally, Homer decides to hire the help of a management company, and their charges amount to 10% per month for managing the property.

So, how much cash flow can Homer expect from his property?

Monthly income: $600 x 2 units = $1200.

Monthly expenses: mortgage = $470, insurance= $50, repairs = $96, taxes = $80, vacancy = $60, capital expenditure = $60, water or sewage = $125, garbage = $50 and management expenses = $120. So, the summation of all these expenses gives Homer a monthly expense of $1111 for the rental property.

Cash flow = total income – total expenses

Cash flow, in this case, is $89 per month.

Cash on Cash Return on Investment

If Homer spends $20,000 to acquire the property, what is the cash on cash return on investment for this property? The annual cash flow a rental property investor receives according to the cash that was invested is referred to as the Cash on Cash Return on Investment. This is a simple method that helps the investor figure out the returns from the property when compared with other forms of investment. The formula you must use to calculate the Cash on Cash Return on Investment is:

Cash on Cash Return = Annual cash flow / the total investment

The total cash flow per year is $1068 (monthly cash flow *12), and the initial investment is $20,000. So, the Cash on Cash Return, in this case, is 5.34% ($1068 /$20,000). Please remember that this rate doesn't include any potential appreciation of the rental property, tax benefits, pay down of a loan, or any other items, which can increase or decrease Homer's profit.

Cash Flow using the 50% rule

There is another quick way in which you can estimate the cash flow using a method known as the 50% rule. As a rule of thumb, it is a good idea to assume that 50% of your rental income will go toward expenses without taking into account the mortgage principal or interest payment. The formula is as follows:

Cash flow = (total income x 50%)- mortgage principal and interest

Let us use the information given in the previous section and determine Homer's cash flow using the 50% method. He is expecting to earn $1200 per month as rent, and the mortgage principal and interest payments amount to $470. When you use the 50% rule:

Cash flow = ($1200 x 50%) - $470. So, the cash flow

is $130. Keep in mind that this is merely a rule of thumb and is certainly not as accurate as a detailed cash flow statement. In this example, by using the 50% cash flow rule, Homer estimates that he can earn $130 per month, but the detailed cash flow statement shows he can earn only $89 per month. Therefore, it is safe to assume that this method is not fully accurate. However, when you are trying to compare and analyze dozens of properties, using this rule will help you decide whether the property can generate positive cash flow or not. Once you shortlist the properties, you can start crunching the numbers and get a fair estimate instead of a vague one.

Chapter 5: Location of The Property

The location of the property is one of the most important criteria when it comes to rental property investing. By opting for an ideal location, the chances of deriving optimal returns from the property increase. However, if you opt for the wrong location, you might get it at a low price and still incur losses. Real estate tends to be quite local. An investment location that might work for one person might not be the best location for you. Generally speaking, the location you opt for must appeal to your potential renters while being profitable for you. In this section, you will learn about the different steps you can follow while choosing the location of the investment property.

Big-picture Location Criteria

The process of selecting the location of the investment property is similar to using Google Maps. You will start with a zoomed-out view of the entire country or the world. Form the bird's eye view you are presented with, you must consider the major trends which will determine the profitability of the property.

Once you do this, you can then judge the property according to different criteria like the neighborhood, connectivity, school district, and more. At this stage, you must consider some major factors like the ones discussed here.

Jobs and economics

A real estate investment will be profitable only if you get the rent you desire and receive it on time. This means you need renters who have good jobs. For instance, if you invest in a rental property in a one-factory town and the factory shuts down, then your investment is bound to suffer. Why does this happen? The vacancies will increase, the rents will decrease, and you will be unable to sell the property for the best market price. So, it is a good idea to study the job market related to the area you want to invest in. Here are certain factors you must consider for determining whether the job market is strong in the area you opted for or not:

- What is the number of jobs present in the overall market? Is this number increasing or decreasing?

- What is the average salary of employees in those areas? Is this number increasing or decreasing?

- What are the types of jobs available in

the area? Are the jobs low or high-paying ones?

- Is there any diversification of jobs in the market? Are the usual jobs a source of stable income?

Every location will have its advantages as well as downsides. However, if you notice that the overall job market consists of diversified jobs, has diversification of the types of employees, the average pay seems to be increasing, and the rate of unemployment is low, then it is a good market. You can also obtain information about the same factors discussed above by going through the local newspapers to find out any plans for development in that area.

In the US, if you want to gain information about the job and local economies, then there are a couple of sources you can use like the Chamber of Commerce, BLS.gov, the Comprehensive Annual Financial Report, and the Comprehensive Plan of the city.

Population growth

Another factor that you must consider is population growth. It is intricately related to the jobs and economics of the region. It is normal human behavior to move to those areas that offer better job prospects. However, there are different factors like weather, local politics, housing rates, and natural attractions that contribute to attracting people to a specific location. While thinking about investing in rental properties, you must opt for a region which shows potential for growth in population. When the population increases, the demand for housing tends to increase, too. Remember, if the supply is fixed while the demand increases, then the commodity value increases. So, if there is an increase in demand and the supply of housing properties is limited, then it leads to an increase in the rental value of the property.

Price-rent ratio

The price-rent ratio helps evaluate whether the property has any potential of being profitable or not. You must divide the average housing price prevailing in the area by the average rent. If the price-rent ratio is quite high, then it is usually not a good market to invest in. Ideally, this ratio should be between 5 to 8. However, this is not the only factor you must consider. Also, if the price-rent ratio is quite low in a specific region, maybe it is low for a reason. So, you need to do the necessary research before you come to any conclusions about whether the property is a good investment or not.

Small-scale Location Criteria

Real estate is often a local market, and once you cover all the previous criteria, it is time to zoom into the neighborhood. Here are certain characteristics you must consider while deciding whether a property in a specific neighborhood is a good investment or not.

Convenience

One of the first things you must consider while selecting a property is the convenience it offers. The best way to go about it is to check whether there is a major economic center within ten miles of the property. I know it might sound quite specific, but you must keep this in mind. Now, you might be thinking that it isn't necessary that everyone has to live within a ten-mile radius from their place of employment, shopping centers, or other community centers. Well, take a moment and think about it - if it were possible to live within a ten-mile radius from your place of employment, wouldn't you opt for this instead of living somewhere that's 20 miles away? Most people would prefer this option. You must remember the equation of demand and supply. As an investor, you must give yourself the best chance at becoming an owner of a successful investment where most people would want to live.

Romance

Wait, what has romance got to do with the investment? I am referring to the fuzzy and slightly palpable criteria that attract people to a certain location on an emotional level. After all, selecting a place of residence is often an emotional decision as much as a practical decision. For some places, romance can include the following:

- Streets that are lined with mature trees forming canopies.

- The proximity to parks or any open spaces where people can relax and unwind.

- Quaint coffee shops, restaurants, pubs, and other eateries.

- Picturesque views of mountains, forests, water, or any other scenery.

- The proximity to commercial districts.

The concept of romance is quite subjective, and it will differ from one location to the next. So, it is time to wear your boots and go scout the location for yourself. Now is the time to explore the location for yourself and see what appeals to you. You must make it a point to physically visit the potential locations to see what you like and what will attract your target customers. You must do this even if you are investing in a property in another state.

Crime rates and safety

Regardless of which part of the world you are based in, you will want to live in a safe location with extremely low or no criminal activity. Well, your tenants aren't any different. As a potential landlord, you must understand that crime can cost you money. Imagine the loss you stand to bear if your property is vandalized, if something is stolen, and so on. Not just that, prospective tenants will also be wary of living in an area with a high crime rate. The local crime rate is often difficult to reverse and therefore, I suggest that you stay away from such locations even if the financials look rather appealing on paper. So, how can you obtain the data you need about the crime rates? The first thing you can do is perform a quick online search using different websites like trulia.com maps, spotcrime.com, city-data.com crime reports, or even by performing a simple Google Search. Once you perform the online search, you must go visit the neighborhood. A couple of red flags you must look out for are bars on windows, protective covers for the HVAC units, and even boarded houses. You can talk to the residents of the area, other landlords, and property managers. Apart from this, you can also visit the local police station to inquire about the crime rate in a specific location.

School districts

Since you are interested in investing in rental properties, you must consider the proximity to school districts. It is an important criterion, especially if your target audience includes families. As with the crime rate, a good place to start your research while looking for school districts is the greatschool.com. However, your decision must not be solely based on online research. You must inquire about the same by talking to local real estate agents. They can provide information about the most popular areas according to school districts among the residents. It is all about getting to know the market you want to invest in and the local situation.

Public transport

In an urban area, the proximity to public transportation like buses, trains, and subways is important while selecting the location of the property. If your potential audience uses public transit, then you must concentrate on those areas which offer good public transport connectivity. I suggest you look at maps of the routes that offer connectivity to your chosen location. A simple search on Google Transit can help you find the available public transportation routes around the world. While using such tools, you must also identify the proximity of bus stops and subway stations from the property. Even a 5-minute longer commute can influence the desirability of the property.

Neighborhood covenants

Most of the neighborhoods and apartment complexes tend to have a set of covenants and conditions along with restrictions which dictate what is and isn't acceptable for the residents. While investing in a property, you must consult with a lawyer or an agent to understand all these rules and regulations. The neighborhood covenants, conditions, and restrictions, or the CCRs, are in place to prevent residents from doing things like placing their old and obsolete vehicles in the front yard. On the downside, they can also stop you from renting the property. At times, CCRs also restrict renting out of properties in certain neighborhoods. That is something you must be aware of ahead of time if you want to invest in a rental property!

Apart from the CRRs, some properties also tend to be a part of a local homeowner's association or a condominium association. These associations are non-profit organizations created by the property owners for the enforcement of the CCRs and the maintenance of the common areas. As a prospective homeowner, you will, by default, be a member of the homeowner's association and will need to pay an annual membership fee. The fee can vary from one place to another, so you must inquire about the same since it is a recurring expense on the property. While purchasing a property, you must do thorough research about the CCRs and the homeowner's associations. At this stage, I suggest you steer clear of all properties with excessive fees and extremely restrictive rules which don't provide the necessary value to the homeowner.

Local laws

The laws of local governments - state, county, or city/town - can influence your investment decision. Here are a couple of things you must pay attention to:

The property taxes - are the taxes payable high or low in relation to the rent? Are the local government entities managing their funds properly? Is there a steep and periodic increase in the taxes payable, or are the rates stable? You can refer to the city's comprehensive annual financial report to analyze these factors.

Municipal services - are the property taxes being used to provide necessary municipal services like picking up trash, keeping the streets clean, access to water and drainage, police and fire services, along with the enforcement of the local laws?

Rental license and laws - the local regulation of the rental properties is a trend that's picking up these days. In some areas, the property owners are required to have a rental license, pay an annual fee, and meet the property inspector at the property once every year. These things take up some time and money. Rental laws relate to basic guidelines about the property being equipped with smoke detectors and such. For instance, in some cities, there exists a law which says that if the owner wants to sell the property, then the first right to purchase is given to the tenant.

Rent control - some cities also have certain rent control measures in place that dictate the maximum rent you can charge for a unit or the rent increment you can charge during a specific period. This is something you must pay attention to, since your earnings from the property are subject to rent control laws.

Eviction laws - the government regulates the landlord and tenant laws in the US. Some states tend to be renter-friendly, while the others are landlord-friendly. If you wish to buy a property in a tenant-friendly state, then be prepared for certain extra costs and time you must spend while evicting a bad renter.

You can obtain all this information from the local government's website. Also, you can inquire about the same by calling or visiting a local code enforcement office and asking them about all the relevant laws a potential investor must be aware of.

Barriers to supply

A barrier to supply is one factor that a lot of investors fail to discuss. It is a simple analysis that can help you increase your earnings as an investor. Remember the rule of supply and demand I discussed at the beginning of this chapter? Most of the criteria related to the location of the property tend to affect demand. It means they tend to influence the number of people who might want to rent your property. However, the barriers to supply tend to affect the number of competing units that can be built in the area. The more difficult it is for a new developer to build new units in the area, the greater will be the value of your rental property in such areas. Here are a couple of things you must look for which tend to restrict supply.

- Certain natural borders which prevent any future expansion like lakes, oceans, rivers, or mountains.

- Human made borders that obstruct expansion like protected parks, land, or universities.

- Any rules which restrict the development of land or make construction activity more difficult and expensive.

- Any zoning laws that limit the

construction of certain types of properties.

Now that you are aware of the different things you must consider while selecting the location of the property, you must start using the same while determining an ideal location.

Chapter 6: Rental Property Management Strategies

Types of Management Strategies

There are three types of rental property management strategies you can use, and they are as follows.

- Do-it-yourself approach

- Half and half approach

- Outsource the management entirely

The type of management strategy you opt for will depend on the resources available to you - essentially, time and money. Apart from this, your level of experience, as well as the proximity to the rental property, can influence your choice of management strategy. In this chapter, you will learn about these strategies in detail.

Do-It-Yourself Approach

As the name suggests, in this type of management strategy, you will be responsible for everything related to the rental property. You will need to collect the rent, pay the necessary taxes, and take care of all aspects of maintenance of the property.

There are two advantages this method offers. It gives you complete control over your investment property. As a small business owner, having complete control over the operations is a nice advantage. When you take care of all aspects of management, you will become aware of all that's going on in the business. Since you will be taking care of the daily management work, you will be able to detect problems right away. Early detection can help fix the problem quickly and prevent it from recurring.

On the downside, you might not have the necessary knowledge to take care of all aspects of management. No one is an expert at everything. There might be some things you can take care of by yourself and others you might need some help with. For instance, if you hire the services of an accountant instead of doing the taxes by yourself, the accountant might discover certain deductions you weren't aware of. Instead of preparing the rental agreement yourself, if you hire a lawyer to help you with it, the result might be a watertight agreement. Also, hiring professionals will ensure you are getting your money's worth and more. It is always better to hire a handyman to fix any repairs instead of doing them yourself. Since you are wholly and solely responsible for the maintenance and the management of the property, everything rests on your shoulders. It can feel like an overwhelming responsibility to take on, especially for someone who is just getting started. Apart from this, when you try to do everything by yourself, you might make certain mistakes or overlook certain aspects of the business.

This form of management is best suited for landlords who need to look after limited rental units, who have some previous business experience or have managed rental properties in the past, and those landlords who want to have complete control over their property.

Half and Half Approach

While following this method of management, you can manage all those areas that you feel comfortable handling or have the necessary expertise to manage and outsource the rest. This method helps you stay involved in the day-to-day operations while ensuring you get the necessary professional help to take care of all those aspects of management you aren't comfortable handling or don't have the knowledge about.

You can outsource the legal aspects along with the maintenance duties. For instance, you can outsource any issues of rental management related to legal matters. You might be good at managing the finances related to the property, taking care of the daily maintenance work, and managing the complaints, but might not be comfortable while dealing with any legal issues. This can include tasks like drafting a rental agreement which complies with all the necessary laws, or dealing with an eviction process. For such things, it is better to hire a lawyer instead of taking on a responsibility you cannot deal with. You can also outsource the maintenance work, like hiring a handyman or appointing a building superintendent for attending to all the significant maintenance issues while you deal with the other aspects of management.

The benefits of this method are that you will have plenty of time on your hands, since the burden of all the tasks doesn't rest solely on your shoulders. This comes in handy if you want to use the rental property for generating passive income while holding onto your day job. You can use the additional time to do things you like or work on other investment options. Apart from this, you can hire experts to tend to those matters beyond your area of expertise. So, you can ensure that you get the best possible help. The only disadvantage is that you rely on others and must trust that they know what they are doing while they keep your best interest in mind.

This strategy is ideal for all those landlords who own several rental units and are looking to expand their rental units.

Outsourcing Everything

If you are interested in becoming the owner of a rental property but have no desire to manage it, then this is the best option available. By opting for this strategy, you no longer have to worry about being a hands-on manager. If you feel like you are a better investor than manager or if you don't have the time to spend managing the property, then this is a good idea. When you hire a property manager or avail the services of a property management company, then they will take care of all steps of property management like screening the prospective renters, collecting rents, maintenance and repair works, tenant eviction and so on.

The most important advantage of this method of management is that it frees you from the trouble of managing the property. You no longer have to worry about attending to a tenant's complaint about a noisy neighbor at 2 in the morning. Your responsibilities as far as managing the property will be down to the bare minimum. Also, you don't have to worry about finding new tenants or evicting a troublesome renter.

On the downside, this form of management can be rather expensive and will eat into the profits you earn from the rental units. The more units you own, the higher will be the cost of outsourcing. Apart from this, another obvious disadvantage is that you will be placing your business in the hands of others. If the person in charge mismanages the property, then it can cost you dearly. Also, if they don't have your best interest in mind while doing their job, it will do you more harm than good. So, you must ensure that you are thoroughly screening the manager or the management company you wish to hire. You must keep an exit strategy on hand to ensure that you can cut your losses and exit the market when things go bad.

This management strategy is ideal for all those landlords who don't live near the rental property, who have a large number of units to take care of, and those who are looking to diversify their investment portfolio.

Steps of Self-Management

An experienced investor might tell you that managing a rental property by yourself is similar to managing a full-time business. For all those owners who want to earn the rent from the property without having to deal with the tenant's complaints, taking care of the repairs and maintenance work on the property and other related works, then hiring a property manager is the best option available. However, by hiring a property manager, you will be increasing the expenses involved. In spite of all the benefits it offers, a lot of investors don't like the idea of incurring additional costs by hiring a property manager. If you happen to be one of those investors, then the good news is that you can learn to manage the property by yourself. In this section, you will learn about the different steps you must follow if you want to self-manage the rental units without hiring a property manager.

The correct rent

The first step is you must decide the right rent amount for the property. The rent you fix must strike a balance between increasing your income and ensuring the property is always occupied by good tenants. The correct rent can be determined by finding the current rental value in the market or by comparing the rent of other similar properties in the chosen area. When you hire a property manager, this responsibility is transferred to that individual. However, you can do it on your own by doing a little research. There are certain factors which can affect the monthly rent like the number of bedrooms and bathrooms, the different amenities and utilities you provide like gas, internet, or water, whether pets are allowed or not, any additional aspects like a garage facility, additional storage, parking space, and backyard, along with the property's location.

Automate the process

One of the major aspects of managing the property is to ensure that you handle and manage all the tasks in an efficient and timely manner. A lot of real estate investors who are self-managing the rental properties tend to invest in rental properties to create an additional source of income. If you want to self-manage, then be prepared to set some time aside for tasks like property inspection, collection of rent, property maintenance, and the processing of applications. If you can automate certain tedious administrative processes, then you can free up some time for yourself. Various online tools and software like Rentec Direct are designed especially for the management of rental units and help streamline tasks like rent collection, tracking the income and expenses related to the property, screening of tenants, and the marketing works of any vacant units.

Learn the landlord-tenant laws

The laws related to rental housing are established for protecting the interest of landlords as well as tenants. Being aware of all the necessary federal, state, and local laws and compliances is quintessential. Ignorance of the law is not an excuse, and non-compliance with laws can land you in legal trouble. NOLO is a good platform to get started with while researching all the necessary laws and compliances. The US HUD (Department of Housing and Urban Development) governs the regulations related to discrimination and other issues that affect the rights of tenants. You can also check with the local and state real estate boards to learn more about these laws.

Diligent screening

A good tenant will not only take care of the property, but will also pay the rent on time. So, if you wish for smooth sailing as the owner of rental property, then you must concentrate on selecting good tenants. You need to establish a good screening process to ensure you weed out any bad renters and are left with only the good ones. Landlords have certain preemptive rights about renting the property to tenants based on their credit score, rental history, and other factors provided in the rental applications and screening reports. Tenant screening is a very important step, and it helps protect the owner's investment. You will learn more about the screening process in the subsequent chapters.

Legal agreement

It is always better to have a written document instead of relying on a verbal contract. Having a watertight rental agreement is your strongest ally while defining your expectations as well as those of your tenant. A legally binding agreement comes in handy when disputes arise. A good rental contract must clearly outline all the terms and conditions of renting out the property along with the rights and responsibilities of the tenants and the owners. Each state has different laws about the landlord-tenant relationship. So, you must go through those laws while drafting the rental agreement. Make the document as specific as you can and don't make it vague or generic. Also, get the document reviewed by a lawyer to ensure that all the compliances are in order and you aren't contravening any laws.

Property maintenance

Routine and seasonal management of the property, along with regular and emergency maintenance, are important aspects of property maintenance. You must stay on top of it to ensure that your property is protected. As a landlord, you are legally duty bound to ensure that the property is always in habitable condition. It means you must strive to create a safe and habitable condition. It isn't merely about fulfilling your legal obligations, but you must do this to ensure that your tenants are happy. Happy tenants mean less turnover and better rents.

Performing regular inspections

If you want to make sure that your property is being properly maintained, then you must conduct regular inspections. There are two benefits to conducting regular inspections. If there are any maintenance issues, then you will be able to identify them during the inspections and take the necessary action to fix them. It also helps ensure that your tenants are sticking to the rental agreement and are taking reasonable care of the property. If you are self-managing the property, then you must conduct regular inspections, apart from conducting an inspection at the start and termination of the rental agreement.

Insurance is a must

There are insurance policies that are designed for specific needs of a landlord, like protection against any financial loss from the rental property or any other financial obligations related to the rental property. Some owners seem to assume that they can use a regular homeowner's insurance policy to cover the rental unit. However, the coverage offered by such policies is often limited and not sufficient to fully protect your interests. The insurance policy you opt for must cover all the likely liabilities and damages related to rental accommodations.

Tax time

Taxes cannot be overlooked or ignored. By investing in real estate, you will be entitled to certain tax deductions and benefits. You will be allowed to deduct certain expenses like insurance premiums, property taxes, depreciation of the property, and maintenance expenses from your total taxable income.

Network

You can join an organization or forum that will help you reach out to other landlords and rental property investors. It not only helps with networking, but you will be surprised by all that you can learn by talking to others. Sharing ideas and advice will help you grow and become a better owner.

Self-managing the property certainly requires a commitment and is a responsibility you cannot afford to overlook if you want to be profitable. So, keep the steps discussed in this chapter in mind while self-managing the property.

Chapter 7: Financing Options

A lot of people are usually surprised by the economics of the turnover between rental properties and stock returns. How can a rental property do better than conventional stocks while having a lower level of volatility and risk? Doesn't a high turnover usually imply greater risks? The answer is quite simple: unlike trading in stocks, the entry barrier to investing in rental properties is higher. Anyone can start investing in the stock market with capital as low as $100. It is one of the significant advantages of investing in the stock market, regardless of its volatility. However, when it comes to investing in rental properties, the returns are high, and the risk is comparatively low. There are two challenges a potential rental property investor must face, and they are the high capital required to acquire the property and the skills necessary to manage the investment successfully. Up until now, you were provided with information about how to select a property and analyze it; in this section, you will learn about the financing options available to you.

A down payment on the rental property is a significant expense you will incur. However, there are certain financing options you can use without having to worry about a down payment. These options are as follows.

House Hacking

The simplest and perhaps the easiest way in which you can buy a rental property is house hacking. A significant advantage of this option is that you can pay for the property while living in it for free. The concept is rather simple: you buy a multifamily unit and occupy one of the units while you rent the other units. The rent you get from the other units will help pay for the mortgage and other housing expenses, while you get a place to reside. Also, when you finally move out, the property will still function as a rental unit, and your cash flow will increase.

Are you wondering how this will help with the down payment? A mortgage lender will charge a much lower down payment on a property that's occupied by the owner when compared to other investment options. It is based on a simple risk calculation - the chances of a borrower defaulting on a loan on their own home is lower than the chances of default on a loan needed for rental property. A very popular loan option with an extremely low rate of a down payment is the FHA

(Federal Housing Association) loan that requires a down payment of only 3.5%, provided your credit score is more than 580. If your credit score is less than 580, then I suggest you work on paying off the existing debts before you think about investing in a rental property.

FHA is not the only option available, and in fact, there are certain loan schemes which require a smaller down payment, or even no down payment altogether. So, you must inquire about the different mortgage schemes provided by at least three different local lenders before you choose your financing option.

Seller Financing

Wait a moment - who says that you need to opt for a loan to finance the rental property investment? At times, the sellers offer to finance the property for you, and you can negotiate terms with the property's seller. This means you can negotiate a deal sans any down payment. This is a good option when the seller has no mortgage or when the property was passed onto the seller as an inheritance. Maybe the property might need certain repairs, and the seller doesn't have the funds to pay for them. Often, such sellers are more than happy to accept regular monthly payments for the property and earn the income while quickly settling the property without having to deal with realtors and paying for their commissions. All sellers might not provide this option, but many will, provided you ask them about it. This is certainly an option you must not overlook, especially if you want to purchase a rental property without incurring any down payment.

Assuming the Seller's Mortgage

At times, the seller might not be ready to finance the rental property directly, but you can still acquire it without having to pay much or anything as a down payment. If the seller has an existing mortgage on the property, then you can offer to assume the same and make the mortgage payments. You will essentially be assuming the responsibility of paying off the existing loan. When you do this, you merely need to finance the remainder of the difference instead of worrying about making a hefty down payment.

Whenever you purchase a rental property using conventional financing options, the lender will not allow you to borrow unless you make a down payment. They do this to ensure that you are involved in the game and will make the rest of the payment without any failure. When you purchase a property by assuming an existing mortgage, you will have to make the mortgage payments and pay the seller any difference amount between the actual price of the property and previous mortgage payments made by the seller. You can pay the seller any way you want, such as borrowing the sum from your family or friends or even by using your credit card. You can also try to negotiate a loan with the seller.

Negotiating a Second Mortgage

You could find a lender who is willing to lend you funds equivalent to about 90% of the rental property purchase price. However, if you don't have the rest of the funds, then you can turn to the seller. All lenders don't offer this option, so before you go ahead and negotiate about the seller taking a second mortgage, you must clear terms with the primary lender. If you are opting for an FHA loan, then the option of a seller-held second mortgage is not available.

Collateral-Based Lending

Most of the conventional lenders, as well as FHA lenders, tend to be sticklers for rules. They might not allow you to borrow money from the property's seller or anyone else to allow you to finance the rental property without any down payment. However, every lender is not necessarily this fussy when it comes to the source of the down payment. Landlord lenders, as well as hard moneylenders, tend to lend funds based on the property as collateral instead of the borrower. The advantage of this option is that they aren't concerned with the source of the down payment, as long as it is not them. On the downside, they tend to offer a low loan-to-value ratio;

this means the down payment required to be made will be higher. You must opt for a hard money lender for loans regarding any short-term renovations instead of a long-term loan. If you are investing in a property which can be rented out immediately, then you must look for an affordable long-term borrowing option. When you decide to opt for collateral-based lending from the landlord lender, then you can source the down payment from any other source of your choice like friends, family, the seller, personal loans, or any other source you can think of.

Another benefit of a landlord loan or any other collateral-based lender is that you will not be charged mortgage insurance. It essentially means that even when the interest rate payable is slightly higher, the monthly payments you make will be relatively lower since you don't have to pay for mortgage insurance.

Partners

As I have already mentioned, you can borrow from your family or friends for financing the property. However, who says you must restrict them to the role of money lender only? You can always take them on board as your investment partner. For instance, let us assume that you don't have the funds for a down payment, but you want to learn about investing in rental properties. On the other hand, your friend has the necessary funds but doesn't want to spend any time learning the tricks of the trade. Well, this couldn't have been more perfect. If your friend agrees to become a partner for the rental property investment venture, then they can provide the equity while you take care of the operations. This is a great way for your partner to earn passive income and for you to gain an investment opportunity.

Credit Cards

As with friends and family members, I have mentioned that you can pay using your credit card a couple of times to this point. Using a credit card to meet your financial requirements can be a good idea, since the line of credit is easily available. However, you must understand that most credit cards usually charge a cash advance fee that's anywhere between 3 to 4%, and the interest rate charged by them is quite high, too (around 10 to 25%). On the plus side, this is quite a flexible option, and you can use reward points to mitigate the cash advance fees. For instance, if you need $100,000 to purchase a rental property investment and the landlord is willing to lend you $80,000, you still need to come up with the remaining $20,000. You can use a cash advance from your credit card to finance this $20,000 requirement quickly. The one thing you must concentrate on is paying off the borrowed sum on the credit card as quickly as possible. Remember that the interest rates are quite high and the more you delay it, the greater will be the sum repayable. You are in a race against the clock now. If you think you can repay the borrowed sum within a couple of months, then this is an option you can consider. However, if you think that it will take you a couple of years to repay the borrowed sum, then steer clear of credit card debt.

HELOCs

Another wonderful idea for financing a rental property investment without any down payment is to borrow against your existing residence. HELOCs, or Home Equity Lines of Credit, will serve this purpose. You can gain a credit line against your current residence, and you can draw on it as the need arises. The rental income you earn from the property can be used for paying off the HELOC. Let me continue with the above-mentioned example. If you are borrowing $80,000 from the landlord, then you must secure the remainder of $20,000 to secure the rental property. It is cheaper to opt for HELOC instead of turning to credit cards, at least in terms of the interest rates chargeable. The up-front costs for starting a HELOC will be higher since the lender needs to run a title history on your current property and will charge you some junk fees. A HELOC is like a gift that keeps on giving. You can put it in rotation to buy rental properties, pull money out of it, repay it, and then repeat this process.

There are several reasons why you want to get a HELOC (equity line of credit), for example, to renovate a house, improve a home, or even invest in real estate. Installing a HELOC is not expensive and costs a fraction of the amount you are looking for. You may not need the money immediately. Nevertheless, it is very convenient if there is an excellent investment opportunity coming your way.

The qualifications you need to get a HELOC are very similar to those you need to meet to get a regular mortgage. The bank would require you to have a good credit rating and a good income, which can help you secure the amount for which you are applying. The requirements for all this vary from bank to bank, as well as your credit requirements. You must own the property that you are borrowing against. Capital is the difference between the value of your property and what you owe in relation to that property. Banks have different loan rates and costs. It also depends on the type of property you own (be it an investment or a personal residence).

The variable credit line for private homes is about 2% above that of Wall Street Prime, the minimum rate is 5%, and the maximum rate is 21%. You do not pay monthly or yearly fees, and you only have to pay interest on the money you use from HELOC. The bank must rate the property, and once this is done, the HELOC will be provided after paying multiple fees. With this form of a loan, you have the opportunity to repay the debt anytime that's convenient for you.

Other Options

The easiest way to use less money to buy rentals is to have a cheaper selection of homes. Market prices primarily determine the price of a rental property. You do not have to spend all your money on renting a property. You can buy something for a lower price and then decorate it if you want. You can also purchase rental properties as a renter. This means you can stay in this property for about a year and then rent it out. This technique saves you a lot of money. However, the payments you make for interest on loans and mortgages are higher. Higher fees usually hinder the flow of money from these investments.

Buying real estate for multiple families is another self-serving strategy. If you manage to buy a property that consists of about four parts, you can get a bank sanction to get a loan to a tenant if you live in it. If you wish, you can rent this unit after one year.

You can also reduce the amount of cash you need to buy a rental property by choosing Vendor Financing. One of the problems with financing the seller is finding a seller who is willing to provide you with the necessary credit. The cost of financing from the seller may be higher than your regular bank loan.

Another option is to work with another investor. This means that the amount you invest will be significantly reduced and you will continue to be able to share profits and make decisions. However, make sure that you have an agreement so that there are no unnecessary disputes in the future. An extremely risky strategy is to buy rented property by taking a hard cash loan and then refinancing that property into a traditional mortgage. Of course, to implement this strategy, you need a lot of experience, and it is quite risky.

The easiest way to save money on an investment is to save some of your income directly. You can save up to 50% of your investment income. It's not easy at all, no matter how much you make every month. Both our society and the economy are designed to make it easy to spend and hard to save. If you manage to control your spending habits, you can save more money. This does not mean that you should not spend money or live modestly. It means you have to spend your money wisely.

Saving your tax returns

You can save your tax refunds at any time for future investment. It is not difficult. You can set up your bank account so that when you receive a tax refund check, it will be credited directly to your savings account. That way, you'll make sure that you have not spent that amount on unnecessary things.

Set aside part of your payroll for investment

You can talk to your employer and get them to set aside part of your monthly salary for investment. If you are self-employed, you can instruct your bank to allocate part of your monthly income to real estate investments. You have to keep a certain percentage of your monthly income to live, of course. Depending on your comfort level, you can vary this percentage. It can be as high or as low as you like.

Living modestly

If you want to invest in the real estate market, you will undoubtedly need a lot of money. You can do this by living modestly for a while. Living modestly does not mean accepting a Spartan existence. For a while, you can prioritize your spending. You can set aside all expenses that seem superfluous or wasteful. You might desperately want to buy a pair of Louis Vuitton pumps, but this desire can certainly be suspended for some time. You'll be surprised at how much money you can save by prioritizing your spending. Anything that is not necessary can be delayed.

Additional sources of income

You can start your own business. If you have your own business, you have full control, and the opportunities to make more money are also high. Owning and maintaining rental properties can also be a business. You need to make sure you run the business, and not the other way around. A company should be able to make money for you without much effort.

An easiest way to get more money while you're part of someone else's business is to ask them. If you work for someone and know you are doing well, you can directly ask for a promotion. If you think you have no reason to ask for a pay raise, work harder so you can ask for what you deserve. If you think that you have reached a saturation point in your current job, you may want to consider making a career change. You can turn to what you like and like to do. It is never too late to do what you enjoy and are passionate about. There are different ways that you can make more money by doing what you want, and many of your passions can be turned into hobbies that earn you side income.With this income, you can invest in real estate.

Chapter 8: Exit Strategies

Investing in rental properties is an excellent way to develop a stream of passive income and increase your cash flow, but it is not always easy. It is quintessential that while purchasing a rental property, you develop an exit strategy, too. You never know when you might have to quit the game and to help you do this, you require an exit strategy. Most investors don't pay any heed to this and tend to suffer a loss when they try to get out of the game. It is a good idea to think about how you might need to exit the rental property market and consider this while investing.

You might want to invest in multiple rental properties to substitute your income or add on to your current income. The end goal might be to generate passive income, which gives you the financial freedom to pursue your dreams and maybe even quit your day job. It all sounds quite wonderful, doesn't it? That said, you might wonder why you will need an exit strategy when you like the steady rental income. Well, there might be some reasons or situations which will prompt you to sell the property, and when that does happen, you need an exit strategy.

Here are a couple of reasons why you might want to sell the property:

You might have had some bad experience, like dealing with horrible renters, poor property management and the like. I am certain a lot of people tend to sell their rental properties because of this reason. You need to understand that dealing with a bad renter is a very real possibility and it is just a part of being a rental property owner. A bad tenant can cost you a lot of resources - time as well as money. Appointing a bad property management team can also worsen the situation further and is at times the cause of all the trouble you are facing. It is not easy to find the perfect property management team, and the inability to do this can cost you dearly (if you don't want to self-manage the property). A good property manager makes all the difference in being successful or unsuccessful. I suggest that if you ever come across any such problem, the best thing you can do is fire the property manager or property management team and hope that things will turn around for you.

You might face a personal emergency. Life is full of uncertainties, and misfortune can befall anyone at an inopportune moment. If you are experiencing a personal emergency or a financial crisis, then it might be time to let go of the rental property. This is quite understandable. At times like this, you must concentrate on minimizing the losses by using a good exit strategy. You will learn more about this in the following sections.

Maybe you were looking forward to being a rental property investor, but as time went by, you realized that being a landlord is not meant for you. You might have tried and concluded that you need to quit being one. This does happen, especially when a new landowner tends to take on more than they can handle and manage. If you ever reach this point, I suggest that you give rental property investing another chance and hire a good property manager. Yes, it will eat into your profits, but at least it will help trigger the cash flow.

You might be interested in making a move on to better and bigger investments. This might be the only positive reason why you might want to sell an existing rental property. If you think you are headed toward bigger investments, then you will need to mobilize your finances for the same. If you are at this stage, then don't feel bad about letting go of one investment and instead think of this as progress.

Types of Exit Strategies

Since there are several reasons why you might need to exit from the rental property investment business, it is certainly wise to have an exit strategy in mind while purchasing the property. At times, things might seem peachy on paper, but the reality might be quite different.

To quote Mike Tyson, "Everyone has a plan until they get punched in the face." You might have certain ideas about how the property needs to perform, but you certainly need to have at least one good exit strategy in mind before you even purchase the property. You can change the exit strategy over time, but at least you will be prepared when things don't go as expected. Markets can fluctuate, your fiscal position might change, or even your terms of the loan. A smart investor always has an exit strategy. Here are a couple of good rental property exit strategies you can consider.

Sell

Most rental property owners concentrate solely on the monthly rental income. They tend to spend so many hours crunching numbers and figuring out the monthly ROI that they forget to think about the big picture. It is quite rare that a rental property owner will hold onto the property forever unless it is in a perfect location and the returns from the property will never diminish. The chances of selling the property are quite high. So, the question isn't why you would want to sell, but when you will sell. Are you looking to hold onto the property for a specific period until you can recover your investment? Is there a number at which you might be willing to sell the property at any moment? These questions might seem like something you would consider a couple of years down the road, but you need to answer them right now.

Any repairs or any improvements/ enhancements you do will affect the future value of the property. The decisions you make now will determine the property's value a couple of years later. If you are aware of when and why you want to sell the property, it will enable you to make better decisions in the present.

Own outright

The idea of being able to own the property outright and netting all the rent you receive is quite tempting. However, unless you are willing to part with a rather significant amount as down payment, this will take at least a couple of years to occur. Your plan to pay down or repay the loan must begin with the first payment. You must consider your repayment schedule if you want to be able to own the house outright and as quickly as you possibly can. The more you contribute toward the principle, the easier it will be to repay the remainder of the loan. This strategy will work regardless of whether you opted for a 15 or a 20-year loan. It certainly cannot happen overnight, but think about not having to worry about any repayments. You can use the rental property as a means to secure your retirement. The expenses you will need to pay for will be the property tax, insurance, and any other utilities. If this is your ultimate objective, then you will need to start working effectively toward it from the get-go.

Refinancing

There are a couple of other options available that many rental property owners are unaware of. Rental property loans and schemes have certainly had quite a makeover in recent times. That said, if you have the required credit score and equity, the number of options available to you increases. One option you can use as an exit strategy is refinancing. Loans meant for this purpose tend to have a ceiling rate of 75 to 85% of the loan value, and it depends on the number of rental units. This means the new loan can extend to up to 7% of the appraised value. You must pay off the existing primary lien and hold onto any excess cash to use for any other purpose. If you use it properly, then you can use it to expand your business or even collect it for a future down payment. Either way, if you have the necessary equity but aren't interested in selling the property, then you should consider refinancing.

HELOC

If you want to hold onto the property, then you can add a new home equity line of credit or HELOC. A HELOC functions like a second mortgage in addition to the existing lien. Everything related to the initial loan stays the same, but now you have another loan backing it. HELOCs are unique in terms of the repayment they offer, the rates, and the fees applicable. A HELOC provides the option of only having to repay the interest for the first ten years followed by the repayment of capital for the next ten years. This helps ensure your costs stay as low as possible.

Staying put

At times, the best thing to do is to do nothing. This might sound rather contradictory, but you can hold onto the property even without a specific exit strategy. Now, if push comes to shove, you must be able to act. However, you can give yourself a specific timeframe to evaluate your position. You can evaluate your positioning after a year, at the end of five years, or even ten years. What you must not do is keep making the mortgage payments without having a specific end goal in mind. Take some time and decide what you want to do with the property.

The absence of an exit strategy will prevent you from making sound decisions based on reason and thought. By preparing yourself for the unexpected, you can ensure that you are always a step ahead and nothing catches you unawares.

Chapter 9: Stages of a Screening Process

There are five stages of a screening process, and they are as follows.

- The first contact - This is the step wherein the prospective renter calls you to inquire more about the property or the lease. You must ask some pre-screening questions at this stage to ensure the prospective renter is a genuine one and isn't wasting your time.

- The showing - Once the prospective renter clears the first stage, the second stage is to show the rental property to the renter. This will probably be the first time you are meeting the renter, and you must look for certain red flags at this stage.

- The application - If the prospective renter is happy with the property and you are still interested in renting the property, then the third phase sets in. It is now time to get the renter to fill out an application that includes references from any past landlords as well as the current employers. You must run a credit and a criminal check on the renter.

- Approval process - If the tenant seems to tick off all the right boxes, then you must accept such tenants and decline the offers of the other applicants. Until the moment you sign the rental agreement, the screening process goes on.

- Signing the contract - Once you and your prospective renters are both happy with each other and the property, it is time to make things official. You must sign the rental agreement and carefully go through all the points included in it. You must also ensure that you and the renter agree on all the terms and conditions mentioned in the lease.

These are the five steps of a screening process, and you will learn about them in greater detail in this section.

First Contact

An experienced landlord is aware that nothing can be more troublesome than having to deal with a bad tenant. Essentially, most of the problems a landlord faces due to his or her renters can be avoided by following an effective screening process. If you don't implement certain consistent steps while screening the tenants, then you must start following all the tips given in this chapter.

When to start screening?

The screening process doesn't commence after receiving the rental application or before signing the rental application. In fact, for most rental property owners, it is a good idea to start thinking about screening the tenants from the first contact before showing the property to the prospective renter. The point of the first contact is when the prospective renters approach you through call or email to let you to know that they are interested in the property. There are certain pre-qualifying questions you can ask the interested parties to screen out the bad tenants. You must establish a simple dialogue before meeting the tenant by asking certain questions, which will help gauge the seriousness of the tenant about renting the property.

Questions to include

The first question you need to ask is, "Why do you want to move?" This question might seem like it doesn't concern you, but it does. I suggest you carefully note the answer you receive, because a prospective renter might at times want to move out because he or she is being evicted or due to a poor relationship with the previous landlord. If the prospective renter seems to complain about the existing landlord or their living situation, it is often because they are bad tenants (but not always - there are bad landlords out there, too). Look for prospective tenants who have some legitimate reasons for moving, like needing a bigger residential property or because they are changing jobs and such.

The second question you must ask the renters is, "When are you planning to move in?" If the tenant readily responds with a vague "Maybe tomorrow or even next week", it might mean the tenant isn't that good of a planner. Responsible tenants will start their search for a rental property months in advance in a planned manner. Most landlords usually need a 30-day notice period before a tenant moves out. If you feel that the timing will not work for you, then you don't have to show the property to the renter.

The third question you ask must be related to the monthly income of the potential tenants. The basic idea is to find renters who earn about 2.5 to 3 times the rent payable. This is just simple math, which will help figure out whether the prospective tenants will be able to pay the rent promptly. Once you inquire about this, the next question you must ask them is whether they will have the security deposit along with the first month's rent ready upon signing the rental agreement. This will help evaluate the renter's financial health. Steer clear of those tenants who offer to pay the security deposit in installments.

The next question you must ask is related to obtaining any references from their previous landlords and employers. If the potential renters cannot provide the necessary references or keep making excuses, then don't hold your breath unless the potential renter is just shifting from their parent's home for the first time. Once you receive the references, you need to do your due diligence. Also, while asking for references, ensure that you are asking for a former landlord instead of an existing one.

The final question you must ask is about whether the potential renters will be willing to provide a rental application and give their consent for a credit/background check or not. The answer to this question must be either yes or no. Any candidate who says no must be immediately disqualified. If someone doesn't want to comply with a credit or background check, it is usually because they have a spotty record. You must not ignore such instances.

There is one bonus question you can pose, and that's related to the number of people who will be living in the rental property. You might have to adjust the rent, the security deposit, or even restrict the number of people who can reside in the property. Most states have laws which say that a valid lease cannot allow more than two people per bedroom.

If you plan on asking these questions over a phone call, then quickly jot down the answers you receive and compare them with what the potential renter included in the rental application. If you notice any differences and discrepancies in answers received from this stage and the one where the rental application is submitted, it is an obvious red flag. Also, there are certain things you must keep in mind while dealing with the replies you receive from the renters.

- You must not make up your mind during this interview unless it is about paying heed to certain red flags.

- You don't have to make any exceptions because the potential renter is telling you a sob story.

- You must never make a decision based on such sob stories.

- You must always ask them for a credit report; you cannot overlook this step.

Show the Property

Once you are happy with the answers of the prospective tenants in the previous step, it is time to move on to the next step. The second step of the screening process is to show the property to the potential renters. While you are showing the property to them, it gives you a chance to evaluate things for yourself quickly. Also, you will learn about certain red flags you must pay attention to in this section.

Tips to follow

While showing the property, your main aim must be to get the prospective tenant to convert into a definite tenant. You must make the tenant want to rent your property. Not just that, you must also concentrate on finding good tenants. Here are certain tips you can use while showing the property:

You must consider the property's curb appeal. It means you must ensure the hedge around the curb is well maintained and trash is not lying around. Debris and overgrown hedges will make a prospective tenant wary about renting the property. The first impression of the property does matter. If you are aware of any existing problems in the property, then please get them fixed before you show the property to the renters. You must take care of any leaky faucets, paint that's peeling off, a pest infestation or any other problems that the renter might notice. When a potential renter sees a messy property, that person might conclude that it is okay to mistreat the property since the owner isn't interested in taking care of it.

You need to have certain selling points about the property on hand that you can discuss. Talk about the large bedrooms, the amenities offered, storage space, and any other features you can think of. You might not have considered yourself to be a salesperson up until now, but you are certainly trying to sell the property here.

Please turn on the lights and ensure that the prospective tenant can view the property in the best lighting. Apart from this, you need to regulate the temperature to make it pleasant and comfortable. You might also want to prepare yourself by carrying a rental application, authorization forms for background and credit check, and so on.

Red flags to watch out for

You might have often heard that it is unfair to judge a book by its cover. However, in this case, please judge away. This will probably be the first time you have met the prospective renter personally. You can learn about the prospective renters based on how they carry themselves, the observations they make, and the way they respond to you. I know it might sound rather shallow, but this is quintessential since it concerns your ability to earn returns from your investment. The first thing you can do is to pay attention to their choice of vehicle. Does the vehicle look well maintained, or does it look like a mobile dumpster? It is quite likely that the potential renter will treat the property the same way the car is being treated.

You can also observe the family dynamic and meet any others who might be moving in with the tenant. You can also make a note of their manners. Did the tenants wipe their feet before entering, do any of them smoke, and so on? Make a mental note of the positive as well as negative traits you observe. Apart from this, there are certain red flags you must watch out for.

Did more people show up to view the property than the renter had implied or mentioned during the phone call or the email? Please make sure you are aware of who you will be renting the property to. Each renter needs to submit an application and also give you the necessary authorization to conduct a credit and a background check. You must not allow those who are not a party to a rental agreement to live on the property.

Did your prospective renter speak ill about the existing or previous landlords? What are the complaints you kept hearing about? Will you be able to validate such complaints by checking their references? The usual reasons why a landlord-renter relationship turns sour are money and behavioral troubles. These are two things you must not inherit from the renter. Does the new renter seem to be in a hurry to find a property? Unless the tenant has a good reason to justify the rush, it is often a sign of some trouble like an eviction from their current housing.

Did the new tenants turn up on time, or were they quite late? You can use the answer to this question to gauge whether they will be punctual about their monthly rents or not. Was it easy to coordinate with the prospective renters? An ideal situation is one wherein your renter will pay the rent on time and take good care of the property. However, this doesn't happen quite often, and you will need to coordinate with the tenant. You must ensure that the tenant will be able to take good care of the property.

Did you catch your tenants criticizing the property? If they aren't yet renting the property and have already started to complain, it is a red flag you must spot immediately. If the potential tenants are like this before the tenancy, then it will only get worse when they are the actual tenants. Carefully listen to all the questions your new tenants might ask. The questions they ask will help you understand the things that do and don't matter to them. It helps you understand how they prioritize things in relation to the property.

Rental Applications

In this section, you will learn about the essential aspect of the screening process - the rental application. The different topics covered in this section include what must be included in the rental application, who needs to fill it out, and how you can use the information provided by the tenants to make up your mind.

So, who all needs to fill out the rental application? The answer is quite simple - all those who are interested in renting the property need to fill out a form. Apart from this, all those individuals who will be living on the property or are paying a portion of the rent for the property (as is the case with parents paying the rent for their children to stay) must complete the application process. Whenever someone expresses their interest in your property, your prompt reply must be "I need all prospective renters or individuals who are paying a portion of the rent to complete a rental application and even authorize a credit/ background check. So, do you agree to this?"

When you do this, it shows that the rental application process isn't discriminatory, and you are treating all prospective tenants in the same manner. From a business standpoint, it allows the candidates to either select or reject their candidacy for the rental property.

Are you wondering what self-select and self-reject mean? There are two kinds of tenants you will not want to deal with, and you can easily allow them to filter themselves out from the screening process. The first kind consists of such individuals who might be good tenants, but they are not ready to commit to becoming a tenant yet. For instance, if the tenant is just getting started with the process of searching for properties, it is unlikely that the tenant has an answer readily available. Such tenants will need some time to shop around the market, look at different properties, compare the benefits and drawbacks of the properties, and analyze the same before making a decision. They might make good tenants, but dealing with such tenants is usually a futile endeavor. Instead, you can let them know that if they are interested in the property, they need to pay an application fee, and this will weed out such tenants.

The second kind of tenants are the one you don't want to deal with and are bad tenants. The bad tenants tend to filter themselves out of the application process, and you don't have to lift a finger. The rental application you provide the prospective tenants will require all the applicants to fill in all the details. By doing this, the tenants who have a bad credit score or have a history of causing trouble will not want to complete the application process let alone pay the application fee. So, you get to screen the tenants without doing much work. Design the questions such that the tenants will self-accept or self-reject.

Accept and Reject

In this section, you will learn about how to make a decision as far as accepting or rejecting an applicant as well as the traits that make a good renter so that you know when you have made a good decision. You will also learn about the best way in which you can reject an applicant.

There are certain things you can look out for to ensure that you are landing a good tenant at the end of the screening process. The first thing you must understand is that the rental application by itself will not tell you whether a candidate can be a good or a bad tenant. You will need to do some research to reach that answer. By now, I am sure you will have called the previous landlords and employers to learn more about the potential tenant. The employer might have confirmed the tenant's employment, and the conversation with the landlord must not have given rise to any red flags. If you have yet to make these calls, then I suggest you do that immediately. Here are certain things you must look for while searching for a good tenant:

The first thing a good tenant offers is stability. If you have done your due diligence, then you might be wondering what the positive attributes are that you can check for to confirm if the candidate will be a good tenant or not. You need to assess the stability of the tenant. You can do this by checking their duration of employment with the existing employer. Usually, an employee who has been working at a specific place for a couple of years is considered to be stable. If someone stays with an employer for two years or more, it is likely that such a person is looking to develop a long-term relationship with the employer. If the tenant has a stable and steady source of income, then you will receive the rent promptly.

You must check the disposable income of the tenant. It might seem like you are intruding, and it is none of your business. But in truth, it is your business, and you cannot overlook the tenant's earnings. By figuring out the tenant's disposable income, you can check whether such an individual can afford to pay the rent or not. A simple rule you can apply is the three-times rule. If the tenant's income is at least thrice the rent you are charging, then such an individual is a good tenant and will be able to pay the rent.

However, since you were checking the credit score, you can go a step ahead. The three-times rule doesn't consider the other expenses the tenant needs to account for. This is the reason why it is important to run a credit check on the tenant and understand the existing monthly debt payments and see the way it affects the affordability rule. The best rule to follow is the 40% rule. The rule is quite simple, and it states that the rent payable must not be over 40% of the tenant's gross monthly income less all the other debt obligations for the month.

Credit report

Why do you need to obtain a credit report? A lot of landlords skip this step, and it costs them dearly later. Now is the time to use the help of a neutral third-party for performing a check to estimate whether the tenant has a good credit score or not. It essentially helps determine the creditworthiness of a candidate. A lot of landlords tend to skip this step because they don't think of the relationship as they should - as the tenant's creditor. The tenants who agree to move into the property will do so, and in exchange for this, they promise to make a series of payments stretched over a period. You have delivered your end of the bargain, and now you merely need to wait for the tenant to catch up. The tenant will keep paying the monthly dues until the time of renewal of the agreement. This certainly sounds like a relationship that exists between a debtor and a creditor. So, treating the landlord-tenant relationship any different doesn't make any sense.

By using a credit check, you can find out about the debt the tenant has and the reported income to determine whether the tenant can afford the property or not. The total reported income of the tenant minus the monthly debt payments gives you the tenant's disposable income. Does this still look as attractive as the tenant's reported income? You can also check their payment history to see if they are on time with their payments or not. If the tenant isn't usually on time with their payments, then ask yourself whether that is something you can deal with or not. Apart from this, the credit report will also help validate certain items on their rental application.

Sign the Rental Agreement

The last step of the screening process is to sign the rental agreement. In this section, you will learn about the rental agreement and the final chance you have to screen the tenant before handing over the property keys. You will learn about how you can use the process of signing the lease to remove any lingering doubts you have about the renter. You might be wondering what you can do if you have already approved the tenant. Well, it is never too late to tear up the lease and search for another applicant. However, you must do this before the tenant signs the documents.

Reviewing the rental agreement

You must take some time to review the rental agreement with the tenant. You can do this in person or even over the phone. Please start with the most important aspects of the lease like the rent payable, any late fees when rent isn't paid on time, the necessary security deposit, the terms of moving in and moving out, and the rules about the eviction process. If there are any utility fees, pet fees, or any other fees payable, then you must mention these to the tenant. After stating each term, ensure that you and the tenant are both in agreement.

Once you are done discussing the major terms of the contract, you must review all the subclauses mentioned in the document. You must be familiar with all the terms included in the contract, all of your rights, and you should also be able to answer any questions the tenant might have. Then, you must review all the rules and regulations about the lease. Let the tenant know about all the different penalties in place when any of the terms are violated.

When you do this, you give yourself one opportunity to spot a massive red flag - whether the tenant is serious about making this commitment or not. Is the tenant respectful while reviewing the contract? Is the tenant attentively listening to what is being discussed? If yes, then your tenant is quite serious about it. On the other hand, if the tenant seems the least interested in going over all these things, it shows the tenant isn't aware of the commitment or the financial obligation being made. The tenant screening process is not just important because it is a part of the due diligence you must undertake, but it also sets the stage for any future troubles.

Security deposit, first month's rent, and the move-in fees

It is a common practice for the tenant to pay the first month's rent while signing the rental agreement. Also, now is the time to ask the tenant to pay the security deposit along with any moving-in fees. If you are expecting such payments, then you must communicate the same to the tenant while reviewing the contract. The tenant must bring the necessary checks for payment, and you can deposit them after the rental agreement has been signed. To avoid any unnecessary confusion, I suggest you do all of this at least two weeks before the rental agreement kicks in. The first payments you receive are a measure of how the tenant will pay the monthly dues from now on.

The tenants must either carry the payments with them or must deposit them in your account within a couple of days of signing the contract. If the payments don't clear within three days to one week, or if you don't receive the payments within this duration, then don't let the tenants move in. By asking the new tenants to make all these payments, you are essentially gauging whether the tenant has the necessary finances to make the payments or not. Once the rental agreement has been signed, it is considered to be a voidable contract if the payments for the security deposit or the first month's rent don't clear. The tenants made a promise to pay, and since they defaulted on the payment, you can rescind the contract, and the rental agreement will be void henceforth. However, if you do allow them to move in and it is not an issue about whether the contractual obligations have been fulfilled, you can now resort to the tenancy laws and evict the tenant for the non-performance of their obligations.

Setting a deadline

If the tenant doesn't sign the rental agreement onsite when you meet, then ensure that you inform the tenant about the deadline for signing. At times, the tenants might feel pressured and will not want to sign the contract on site. This is quite normal, and you can give the tenant some time to sign the contract. The natural extension given for signing the lease is between 24 to 48 hours. Until the tenant has signed the contract and the payments have cleared, you must not take the property off the market. Also, inform the tenant about this policy.

If the tenant seems to think that the 24 to 48 hour allowance isn't much to review the agreement and sign it, that's a red flag you must watch out for. It means that the tenant is applying for other properties and hasn't decided about the property he or she wants to rent. If the tenant signs the rent agreement elsewhere, then it means it was all a waste of your time. So, whenever a tenant implies that 24 to 48 hours isn't sufficient time, then stick to your guns. You are running a business, and you need to set deadlines to show the tenant that you cannot hold the property waiting for their confirmation and that you too can pursue other applicants.

While going through all the rental applications, you must keep a couple of applicants as a backup. That backup list will certainly come in handy now.

Note: Please ensure that the rental agreement is in compliance with all the local, state, and federal laws that apply. You need to provide all the necessary disclosures in the document. Apart from this, you must also provide any receipts for the payments you receive, like the security deposit and such.

Chapter 10: Increase Tenant Retention Rate

Do you want to increase your return on investment (ROI) from your rental property? If yes, then you must concentrate on reducing the turnover. Turnover refers to vacancy, the period wherein you are not earning any rents but are still repaying the mortgage or a property loan. It isn't merely restricted to the mortgage, but you will need to pay for the necessary maintenance expenses, too. When the property is vacant, and you are searching for prospective tenants, you will need to spend on marketing, advertising, hosting open houses, collecting and processing the rental applications you receive, scanning prospective tenants, and maybe even making calls to their employers or prior landlords for verification. If you employ a property manager, then you will need to continue to pay such an individual even when the property is vacant.

Put simply, turnovers can eat into your bottom line. So, the best way to rectify this is to ensure the property is not usually vacant. The trick is to hold onto your good tenants. In this section, you will learn about different tips you can use to increase your rate of tenant retention.

Understand the Market

You might have a great relationship with your tenants, but if the property is overpriced, doesn't have much connectivity or is outdated when compared to some other property in your area, then the tenants will look elsewhere. While searching for the ideal neighborhood, spend some time understanding the market, too. You must be aware of any real competition in the market along with the rents they are quoting and their reasons for it. Compare other properties to the one you own, and you will be able to get a rough idea of whether your property will fare well or not in comparison. You must step into the shoes of a tenant and think about the various factors that might appeal to them as well as any expectations they might have about the property.

Every couple of months, please go check any vacant rental properties available in your neighborhood. As soon as you enter the property, start thinking like a prospective tenant and make a list of all the different amenities that appeal to you. Apart from this, you can also attend other open houses. If you aren't sure what renters usually look for in properties, then why don't you try talking to a couple of potential renters? Ask them what they think about your property and the things they might want to change.

Also, if you have had any previous tenants, then you must conduct exit interviews, too. Ask them for their feedback about their tenancy, the things they liked, the changes they might want to make, and their reasons for moving out. All of this information will help you get the right read on the property.

List of Improvements

You must learn about all the different improvements a tenant might want to make to the property. This means you must not stop conducting exit interviews or talking with other prospects living in the neighborhood. The best source to understand what the renters want is to talk to them! You can also conduct a semi-annual inspection with the tenants and inquire about all the different changes they would love to make if it were possible. Essentially, you are asking the tenants about what their "dream" rental property is like. Make a note of all the changes they suggest and keep adding to it. You don't have to make all the changes, and be prepared to come across certain outlandish and even ridiculous suggestions. You can make all the changes that are affordable and will help increase the property's value. Make those changes that guarantee a good return on the money you invest.

Once you make such changes, your tenants will feel like they are heard, and their opinions are valued. This, in turn, can make them want to stay put instead of shifting from your property.

Referral Program

If you own several single-family units in a specific neighborhood or have a multifamily building, then here is a simple strategy you can use. Most people like the idea of living near their friends or family members. So, what could be better than being neighbors with the people they love? Announce to your tenants that if they refer the property to their friends or any of their family members, then you will give the friend a voucher to cover the expenses of moving. This is an important point; you must offer the incentive to the person they referred the property to and not the tenant. By doing this, you can easily fill up the vacancies, and your tenants will be happy to have their loved ones nearby.

Screening is Important

You must screen any potential renters before you decide to let out the property. This is one of the most important aspects of becoming a landlord or a property manager. It also has a direct effect on your total turnover. A bad tenant might need to be evicted, or at the very least, you might not want to renew the agreement with such a tenant. By signing a rental agreement with a bad tenant, you merely increase your turnover. It isn't restricted to tenants who don't pay their rent on time or even those who damage the property. You must also screen out any potential house hoppers - those tenants who frequently shift from one place to another. You must look for a stable tenant who will not only pay the rent on time, but will also take good care of the property. It is always a good idea to find a tenant who is willing to stay put for longer if you want to reduce the chances of the property being vacant.

Maintain Reference Files

It is a good idea to maintain reference files. Will you be able to remember important details about your tenants like their occupation, job profile, names of their children, their hobbies, and so on? It is impossible to remember a lot of details. So, create a small reference file for each of your tenants. Add a couple of notes in it about what they do, their birthdate, anniversary, or other important dates. Along with it, make a brief note of every interaction you have with the tenant. Whenever you talk to the renter, even if it is a brief conversation, by recollecting certain details about their lives, you can make the renters feel good.

For instance, it can be something as simple as "Hi, Mr. Smith. How are you doing? The last time we spoke, you told me that John was about to start at a new school. How does he like his new school?" It might sound like a silly thing to do, but by doing this, you can develop a better relationship with your tenant. Your tenants might even be pleasantly surprised that you remember details about their lives, and this ensures friendlier conversations.

Raise the Rent

There are different reasons to increase the rent on an annual basis, even if the hike is a small amount. It helps increase your revenue. Also, you don't want your rent to be lower than the market rate, do you? It helps to increase the rent in small increments instead of giving the tenants notice about a major rent hike.

Don't forget about setting your tenant's expectations - rents will increase every year. Your tenants must expect a slight increase in rents and be assured that they will not have to endure a massive increase in the rent payable. While setting their expectations, you can also offer certain conditions. Whenever the lease is up for renewal, here are three options you can give your tenants:

The first option- they can continue with the month-to-month rent basis with a marginal increase in the rent.

The second option- if they decide to renew the rental agreement for another year, then the rent hike will be less.

The third option is to offer them an option of renewing their rental agreement for the term of two years, where they can lock in that marginal rent hike for the second year.

If the tenants are aware of the fact that the rents will increase, then it will seem like a good idea to lock in a good rental price for the term of two years. This is what I meant by setting expectations.

Pick up the Phone and Call

If you know that a tenant's rental agreement is coming up for renewal, if the rent is late, or if you are filing for their eviction, then you must send a notice. Apart from this, please pick up the phone and call the tenant. According to the law, you must inform the tenant about certain things by sending notices, but it doesn't mean you must stop there.

It is a good idea to talk to the tenant over the phone before they receive formal communication, since the former helps elicit a decent conversation instead of sharp dialogue. If you want to maintain a good professional relationship with your tenants, then make that call and don't put it off. By doing this, you give the tenant a chance to explain their side of the story, too. It gives you a chance to understand why the tenant missed their rent bill. You can always file for eviction, but knowing the reason for it might change your mind.

However, keep in mind that it is a business for you, so always be practical while making decisions.

Don't Barge into the Property

You must always call the tenant before you decide to enter the rental property. This applies to all properties regardless of the type of property. Yes, you must give written notice, but a phone call always helps. Even if it is an emergency, you are duty bound to inform the tenant about your intent before entering the premises. It is a simple way of showing that you respect the tenant's right to privacy. Sure, your property is your asset, and it is your business. To a tenant, the property is their home; learn to respect it. It hardly takes a couple of seconds to make a call like this, and it is a gesture your tenant will appreciate.

Prioritize the Responsiveness

Whenever there is a repair, then please attend to it immediately. If you delay fixing the repair, then the problem will merely fester and can also damage the property. Understand that it is urgent for your tenant, because any problem with their home will be an urgent one. Whenever your tenant reports any problem, ensure that you take action as soon as you can. Always keep a list of contractors handy according to their area of expertise and their costs. If there is any delay at all, please explain it to the tenant, too. When you do this, it shows the tenant that getting the problem fixed is your priority.

Sending Holiday Cards

Make it a point to send holiday greetings to your tenants, at least the "good" ones. If you are thoroughly screening the tenants, then this should include all of your tenants. Sending holiday cards is a good gesture, even more so if they are religion specific. If you know that your tenant celebrates a specific holiday, don't forget to send a holiday greeting. Address the greeting to each member of the tenant's family residing in your property. Try to make the greeting seem as personal as possible. It is not only a good gesture, but will certainly make the tenant feel valued.

Pruning is a Must

No, I am not talking about pruning the lawn. You need to prune your money tree - cut off any dead branches and pluck the rotten fruit. You can use your chosen plant metaphor for this analogy; you do understand where I am going with it, don't you? You need to get rid of bad tenants as soon as you can. Not only are they expensive, but any damage they do the property is an added expense for you. From fixing any damage to filing for eviction to pushing your good tenants to move, you cannot afford to hold onto any bad tenants if you don't want to hurt your bottom-line.

Regardless of how well you have implemented the previous tips, a good tenant will not stick around if their neighbors are troublesome. Each month, look at the rental agreements that are coming up for renewal. If you have your doubts about a specific tenant, send a non-renewal notice as soon as you can. If you have any doubts about holding onto a specific tenant, you already have the answer - you don't. You don't need to look for an explanation or a justification to keep a bad tenant because you don't want to meddle with your turnover. Remember that letting such a tenant stay will do you more harm than good in the long run. If you have good tenants, then it will certainly reduce your maintenance costs, too.

Chapter 11: Mistakes to Avoid

Making mistakes is part of the learning process. However, it is better to learn from the mistakes of others instead of making them yourself. Some mistakes can prove to be quite costly and might land you in hot water. To avoid all this, you must be aware of the common mistakes rental property owners make and how you can fix them. In this chapter, you will learn about such common mistakes along with the ways to avoid making them.

Mistakes to Avoid while Buying a Rental Property

Saving money and investing money tend to be necessary activities for an average individual. By doing this, you can create a financial safety net to fall back on in times of trouble. While saving money, it is quintessential that you carefully consider where you want to park your funds. Essentially, any form of investment you opt for must help you achieve your long-term financial goals. So, it is important you carefully select your stream of investment to grow your capital and increase your income while minimizing the risks involved.

Buying a rental property is one of the best forms of investment. Rental property investment has several advantages and usually offers a rather stable source of income when maintained properly. However, there are a couple of mistakes investors make while purchasing rental property. Here are the mistakes you must avoid making while purchasing a real estate investment property.

Concentrating only on appreciation

New investors tend to make the mistake of investing in a rental property solely based on its appreciation value. Please don't do this. The value of rental properties can fluctuate due to a variety of reasons, and if the market trends don't move like you hoped they would, then you stand the risk of incurring a huge loss. It is a good idea to consider the appreciation value of a property before investing, but it must not be the only criterion for investing. You might have to sell your property unexpectedly, and if the market conditions are not favorable, then you will only incur a loss. Instead, you must concentrate on the cash flow the property can generate. This is why you are required to thoroughly analyze the property and make all the estimates before purchasing. Also, ensure that you are obtaining all the historical data related to the property form the seller while investigating the property you want to buy.

A watertight contract

If you have any assumptions about the property you want to buy, ensure they are all included in writing in the purchase agreement. You must read the purchase agreement thoroughly to ensure it is watertight and no items are missing. While buying real estate, you will need to sign multiple contracts. It is likely that you might not understand all the terms related to it, so you can seek legal assistance for the same. Read the contract carefully, including the fine print, before you sign anything. Make sure all the important clauses and terms are present before signing. An item you overlooked or a missing item can prove to be a costly mistake. Don't hesitate to seek external help and hire a lawyer to help you throughout the process of signing the contract.

Hiring a third-party

Managing the rental property is quite important when you want to get into the business of rental property investing. The property must stay in good condition if you want to reduce your tenant turnover rate. It also helps attract potential tenants. Once you let it out, you must ensure it is being managed properly. Often, an owner might be required to immediately address any repairs or other problems related to the property, such as plumbing leaks, as quickly as possible. If you ignore the problems, it can become an expensive expenditure. Working with in-house property management is a good idea so that the person selling the property is also responsible for the way the investment performs. You do have the option of hiring a third-party service like a property management agent, but it can prove to be quite costly and at times unreliable. The agency you employ might not be fully aware of all the different aspects of property management. Working with an in-house management company is a good idea. Please ensure that the company you decide to employ will be working even during the buying process. If you do have to hire a management company, ensure that you are overseeing their work and aren't leaving everything to them. You are the owner of the property, and any damage to it will eat into your earnings.

Lack of proper insurance

Insurance is quintessential while investing in rental properties. A lack of proper insurance makes your property vulnerable in case of adverse weather conditions like flooding or heavy snow. Failing to buy proper insurance or sufficient insurance is a rookie mistake you must avoid. Insurance needs to be carefully considered and understood while stepping into the world of rental property investing. Any insurance policy you opt for must be accepted only after taking into account different aspects like your financial situation and the location of the property. The insurance policy you purchase will help shield your property from any unforeseeable damage. Also, having the right coverage will indemnify your losses if you suffer any in the case of an unfortunate incident.

Too many properties

Since you are just getting started with rental property investing, it is a good idea to stick to only one investment at a time. Please do this until you get the hang of it. If you invest in too many properties at once, you will not only be spreading your finances quite thin, but you will also be unable to take proper care of all the properties. While getting started with rental property investing, test the waters before you jump into the deep end. Keep in mind that purchasing a home is quite different from investing in a rental property. It is a completely different ball game altogether. I suggest that a beginner must always start with one property, at least initially. By doing this, you will be able to get a fairly good idea of all that's involved. If possible, try to wait for 12 to 15 months before investing in another property. It gives you sufficient time to understand all the technicalities of managing a rental property. Once you decide that investing in rental properties is palatable to you, you can expand your investments. This will enable you to understand all the potential problems that can crop up. Think of the first investment you make as a learning experience to understand the business of rental property ownership.

Owning a rental property is certainly a great means to fulfill your financial dreams and generate passive income. By avoiding the mistakes discussed in this section, you can make the most of your investment.

Common Mistakes Rental Property Owners Make

There is so much more to managing a rental property that goes beyond collecting the rent due. If you are just getting started with owning and managing a rental property, then there are certain things you must be aware of. The most important of all is the fact that you must treat your rental property investment like you would treat a small business. The more knowledgeable you are about proper management, the smaller are your chances of making any costly mistakes. Owning a rental property can certainly be quite exciting, but it can be a difficult pill to swallow if you don't understand what you are doing. So, what are these common mistakes I am referring to? Read on to learn more about these mistakes and how you can avoid them.

Don't try to do everything by yourself

Owning a rental property is quite different from maintaining the property. Becoming a property owner is easy, but managing it can be a rather tricky process, especially if you don't do it properly. Usually, managing a property requires a lot of time, and it is an important responsibility you cannot overlook. The greater the number of tenants you must manage, the more difficult your work will be. Without the proper knowledge, skills, or experience, you might face some difficulties. At times the mistakes can prove to be costly and can land you in legal trouble, too. You can hire an in-house management company to help handle your first investment. While doing this, don't leave everything to them and instead learn the ropes. When you know what you are doing and how to do the job, you can start managing the property on your own. Don't try to do everything by yourself, and seek help when in trouble.

Only a specific service provider

If you do want to hire a property management agency, then you must be aware of the two types of companies - the ones which offer specific services, and the comprehensive service providers. For instance, you can hire a lease management company. It might seem like a good option cost wise, but it is not effective. A company like this will only handle the leases and will not pay much attention to finding good tenants for your property. After all the money you pay for their services, you will need to deal with the tenant whether they are good or bad. Dealing with a bad tenant can be quite stressful. On the other hand, if you hire the services of a management agency providing comprehensive services, then they will not only help you find good tenants but will help manage them, too.

Hiring a real estate agent

Every service provider has his areas of expertise. Even if veterinarians are doctors, it doesn't mean they're qualified to treat humans. Likewise, you must not hire a real estate agent to help you manage the property. Property management is quite different from dealing in real estate. Always approach professionals who provide the services you are looking for. Regardless of how wonderful the real estate agent is, the agent cannot provide you the kind of services a property manager can. Instead of wasting your hard-earned money on a real estate agent who has other priorities, you must hire someone who can get the job done for you. You must not only ensure that you are getting your money's worth, but that the property is well managed, too.

Charging the wrong rent

How you do you know whether you are charging the right rent or not? There are two ways to determine the answer - the first one is when you notice your turnover rates are quite high, you cannot fill the vacancy, and keep getting complaints about the rent being too high. The second method is when your income from the property is less than the income that properties similar to yours yield. Fixing the rent is not an impulsive decision, and you must spend considerable time doing the necessary research and analysis before deciding the rent. If you don't do this properly, then you will incur more losses and not see any profits.

Improper insurance

As mentioned in the previous section, it is quintessential to have the right insurance coverage for your property. Having natural calamity insurance will protect you from incurring any losses during a natural disaster. A lot of new investors don't understand the importance of proper insurance.

Clear rules

Renting a property is a contract you enter into with the tenant. As with any contract, you must set clear and unambiguous rules as well as terms and conditions. If you don't set any clear rules, it can become quite difficult to manage the tenants. The lack of proper rules can land you in unnecessary trouble. This is the reason why you must not only make a list of all rules applicable to the tenancy, but you must also allocate corresponding consequences if the tenant fails to comply. Once all the rules are in place and the tenant signs the rental agreement, both the parties involved are legally liable to follow the rules.

Unhealthy relationships

It is a good idea to have an amicable relationship with your tenants. However, you must also know where to draw the line. Being very friendly with the tenants can make them assume that they can take undue advantage of your friendship. Be friendly while being professional. In the end, you are in business. So, don't forget to treat it like one. If the tenants start to act irresponsibly, then they will only set a bad example for the other tenants.

Repairs and maintenance

A lot of property owners tend to pay for repair and maintenance work by themselves. It might seem like an ideal solution for you, but this is not a good idea in the long run. You might think it is unnecessary to seek outside or professional help with these issues. You must remember that even small maintenance and repair work, if not done properly, can lead to bigger troubles later.

Poor resolution of issues can not only tarnish your reputation as a good property owner, but can even cost you your tenants. If there are any repair and maintenance issues, you must make sure you hire professionals who are competent enough to fix the issue. You own the rental property, and as an owner, the maintenance and upkeep of the property are responsibilities you cannot shrug away. Without the necessary experience, you might forget or fail to do certain things. So, don't try to do the job of a handyman if you have no experience in that field and instead hire help.

By avoiding the mistakes mentioned in this section, you can become a good rental property owner.

Legal Mistakes to Avoid

Being a landlord can be tricky at times, especially for newbies. Here are common legal mistakes landlords tend to make and the tips you can follow to avoid landing in any potential legal trouble.

Discriminating queries

The law prohibits a landlord from refusing to rent a property to a tenant based on the grounds of discrimination like the tenant's race, religion, nationality, sex, disability, familial status, and color. You must avoid asking the potential renters all such questions that seem discriminatory or suggest any intention of discrimination.

Failure to disclose

Different states have different requirements about the facts that must be disclosed. However, there are certain disclosures all landlords must make to their prospective renters. For instance, you must disclose to the tenant any mold that exists if you are aware of it or even have reason to believe that it exists. You must inform the tenants about any registered sex offenders living in the vicinity if you know the same. You must also disclose information related to any recent deaths that might have taken place in the rental property. According to Federal laws, the landlord must also disclose any details about the use of lead-based paints in case the property was constructed before 1978 in the US.

Illegal elements in the rental deed

A rental agreement must not contain any clauses or conditions that violate any laws of the state or any of the Federal provisions. You must avoid including any discriminatory or illegal conditions in the rental agreement like any provision that takes away the rights of the tenant to sue the landlord or the tenant's right to refund. The inclusion of any illegal terms can land you in trouble and make you liable to pay monetary damages.

Provide a safe environment

In most of the states, it is the landlord's legal responsibility to provide the tenants with a safe environment. As a landlord, you are liable to ensure that your tenants are safe from any potentially dangerous conditions on the property and are safe from any criminal activity. You must make the necessary inspections and inform the tenants or anyone else who enters the premises about any hazardous conditions that exist on the property. You must also take reasonable care to ensure the safety of your tenants from other tenants or any other criminals who enter the property. If the tenant sustains any physical harm or the property is damaged and the tenant was unaware of the unsafe environment, then the tenant has the right to sue the landlord. It is all about maintaining a full-disclosure policy when it comes to the property you want to rent.

Refusing to make repairs

While drafting the rental agreement, make sure that you specify the details of making repairs. You must make sure to spell out who this liability rests on. At times, you might have to make certain repairs even when the rental agreement doesn't cover such duties. Every state has laws about having an implied warranty regarding the habitability of the rental properties. A property is considered to be habitable if it provides heating, gas, clean water, is structurally safe (floors and roof), and has plumbing and electricity. If the property is in a state of disrepair, then the tenant has the option to make the necessary repairs and charge it to the owner's account, move out, or even report the apparent violations to a state building inspector. The failure to make the premises habitable is just a lawsuit waiting to happen.

Violating the tenant's right to privacy

The right to privacy is a universal fundamental right, and it applies to your tenants, too. A landlord must not enter a rental unit without giving the tenant a verbal or a written notice 24 hours before entering the premises. A landlord can only enter after giving the notice while repairing, showing the property to any prospective renters, or for the sake of inspecting. If it is an emergency, then this rule isn't applicable.

Eviction rules

As a landlord, you have the right to evict a tenant for not paying the rent, for violating any provision mentioned in the rental agreement, for the failure to vacate on the expiry of the lease, or if the tenant has caused some damage to the property which has led to the depreciation of the property's value. Before you can throw out the tenant, you must follow the due course of an eviction process. Every state has different guidelines about this topic, but a common requirement is that you must serve the tenant an eviction notice before you file a suit for eviction in the court of law. If you try to evict a tenant without following the due process, you are merely attracting a potential lawsuit wherein the tenant can claim compensatory damages.

Withholding the security deposits

Most rental contracts require the tenant to pay a security deposit for any potential damages caused by the tenant or due to the tenant's carelessness. Once a tenant moves out, you can use the amount of the security deposit to fix any damage thus caused. If you do this, then you are duty bound to provide the tenant with an enumerated list of all the necessary repairs and deductions you made and return any balance to the tenant. If you don't provide an itemized list of deductions or fail to return the remainder of the security deposit, you might be liable to pay monetary damages to the tenant.

Deal with abandoned property

If the tenant moves out but leaves certain items behind, then the landlord can treat it like abandoned property. The first thing you must do is notify the renter about claiming such property, the cost of storage if any, where to claim it from, how the property can be claimed, and the duration within which such claims must be made. If the property is unclaimed even after your due diligence, then you can sell the property after issuing a notice about it in the local newspaper if the property is worth more than a specific sum. If the property is below the state-specific limit, then you have the option of either retaining or discarding the property.

Inadequate insurance

Apart from insuring the property for any damage due to natural disasters, you must also insure it against any lawsuits initiated by the tenant. If you evict a tenant illegally, enter the property illegally, or if the tenant or any other person who is legally present on the premises is injured due to a hazardous condition, the insurance will help cover the costs of litigation or any legal action brought against you.

Keep these simple provisions in mind to prevent any legal trouble.

Conclusion

I want to thank you once again for purchasing this book. I hope it was an informative read.

You might be quite excited at the prospect of investing in rental properties now. One of the ideal investment choices you can make is to invest in a rental property. You might want to invest in rental properties for different reasons. Regardless of your reasons, investing in rental properties can be quite lucrative if you are diligent and invest carefully. Armed with all the information given in this book, you can now make informed decisions. You no longer have to seek other sources to learn about rental property investing. The information given in this comprehensive guide will help you get started with rental property investing.

So, all that's left for you to do is get started as soon as you want! While making any investment decision, please ensure that you carefully analyze the risks involved and the returns you can gain. Don't be in a hurry and do your due diligence. A little extra effort can indeed go a long way when it comes to investing. Once you successfully set up the rental property and lease it out, you can start earning passive income.

By following the simple steps and tips given in this book, you can attain the financial freedom you always dreamt of and wished for. The key to turning your life around is in your hands. So, act immediately and make the most of the resources available.

Real Estate Investing – Flipping Houses

Complete Beginner's Guide on How to Buy, Rehab, and Resell Residential Properties the Right Way for Profit. Achieve Financial Freedom with This Proven Method

Introduction

At some point, you have probably heard people talk about real estate investment. For many people, it is an easy way to make money, especially when it comes to flipping houses. Maybe your interest was triggered by shows about flipping you saw on television, or you have a close friend who is earning a lot of cash from real estate. Now, you are interested in going into the business, but you don't know where to begin.

The fact is, lots of other people have been in the same place you are right now. Even worse, many of them were unable to attain success when they finally gave it a try, while some were able to hit the right buttons and become successful in real estate. So what was the difference? Why were a few of them successful, and others were flops? How can *you* be among those successful individuals?

Here's the thing: you are already on the right path. By buying this book, you have taken a significant first step. In this book, you will learn all you need to know about investing in real estate and rehabbing homes. You will also learn how to find the best home to flip and how to get the financing you need.

With this book, you will develop the knowledge you need to buy, rehab, and sell properties for profit. We will look into these topics and a host of others related to real estate investment. I do not promise that there won't be obstacles on the way. However, I am confident that when you are through with this book, you will have a comprehensive understanding of all you need to know to become a prosperous rehabber. Also, if you effectively use all the information offered by this book, you will be able to sell your first home and many more for continued profits.

Now, let's begin this journey to becoming a successful real estate investor.

Chapter 1: Basic Concepts

House Flipping: What is it?

House flipping is when an individual makes the choice of buying a property to fix it up and quickly resell it. The individual buys the property and raises the value by renovating it before selling it for profit within a few months.

There are two major kinds of real estate investment you will be coming across as an investor in real estate, which we will discuss below:

Wholesale Flipping

Wholesaling has to do with buying a property and reselling it to another investor immediately, for a profit. This mostly takes place the same day or at the same closing table. Here, you rarely have to do any form of repairs on the property before selling it to some other investor.

As a wholesaler, you are only reselling the same property you purchased, but for a profit. If you want to be successful as a wholesaler, you must be excellent at negotiating and should be able to persuade sellers to let go of properties at a price lower than the market value, while still convincing buyers to buy at higher than the market value. As a wholesaler, you sell homes for a profit in only a few days, which means you get faster paydays and the possibility to engage in more deals than those involved in other forms of investment.

Although wholesaling is fast, there are a few downsides to it. First, you need to have investors on hand who are willing to buy your property. When it comes to wholesaling, the absence of a ready buyer means no deal. Also, based on how you drew your contract and the amount you placed in escrow, you might need to pay back your seller if you have problems finding a buyer. It is ideal to have prospective buyers ready before you make the seller an offer. This way, you have a lower risk of losing cash. Sometimes, the money you lose might substantial, but the primary damage would be to your reputation. If the news reaches others that you have a negative impact on homeowners, others may not be interested in collaborating with you. If you feel wholesaling is not ideal for you, there is a more common type of real estate investment, known as rehabbing.

Rehabbing

Rehabbing is when an investor buys a property, renovates it and upgrades it before selling it for a higher price. These projects have a life span of four or more weeks, depending on the level of work that needs to be completed during the renovation. The process is also known as "fix and flip," and it is one of the most popular methods of investing in real estate today, and not without good reason. Rehab properties can provide investors with a considerable profit margin while also aiding them to expand their network and portfolio.

Property owners who renovate their homes to increase the value of the property or for personal use, also fall under the category of rehabbing. This is the case even if they have no plans to sell off the property.

There are a host of other methods to flip homes beyond rehabbing and wholesaling; however, these are the most popular. In comparison to wholesaling, there are a lot of more options open to a rehabber, that will provide a broader opportunity to get returns. With this in mind, the rest of this book will pay more attention to the rehab aspect of flipping homes.

How Does House Flipping Work?

To flip a property the right way involves a reasonable amount of work. You need to follow a few steps which will be discussed below:

- Find: Search for properties that will make fantastic deals. Here, you are on the lookout for people who have an interest in selling their homes. There is a range of reasons individuals want to sell their homes. For a few of them, selling the house can help them fix a pending challenge, while for others, the home may be a problem they want to get rid of. Your objective should be to find these people and help them solve their problems. However, you need to have a budget and be aware of the highest amount you can invest in buying a property.

• Search for Financing: Next, you will need to look for a way to finance your house flip. With this, you will be on the lookout for lenders who can provide you with funding based on the value of the property. If you have the capacity, you can invest your own funds.

• Renovate or Fix: The next step in the process is to renovate or repair the home. This is the step that separates those who are successful from those who fail. To properly do the job, you need to pay attention to contractors, monitor the cost of repair, and remain within your timeframe and budget to develop homes people will want to buy. You also need to have a knowledge of negotiation with contractors and how to pay them the right amount to ensure they will do the job right.

- Flip: If the process is followed correctly, you will have a completed property at a reasonable price. This is the period you advertise your home for sale and learn ways to sell to make sure you get a good profit on your investment.

How Much Can You Make Flipping?

You can earn a lot from flipping homes, especially if you invest these returns into flipping more properties. The more places you flip, the more your profits will keep rising. If you check out what flippers earn per flip, you will see that house flippers are not just talking, they are making a tremendous amount of cash.

In the United States, the aggregate profit margin for flipped homes is $29,342 ("The Average Gross Margin in a House Flip", 2018). Although this is a pretty decent profit, you will be able to make more profit if the properties you are flipping sell in the range of $100,000 or more. These properties come with a 54 percent ROI, which makes it the most lucrative price range for house flipping.

The amount of money you can make from flipping a property is also dependent on where you are located. In 2013, flippers in Massachusetts made a gross profit of $103,384 on each home on an average, while flippers in California pulled in $99,999 for each property in 2013. New York, New Jersey, Maryland, and Washington are also states that have helped flippers make lots of profit ("6 Best States to Flip a House in USA – Oracle Fields", 2018). If you can flip a home in one of these states, then you will be able to make some serious cash on each flip.

Even though there are average earnings, you have the potential to make more of this or way less, depending on your skills. You need to understand the rate of success and failure before you head into this business. However, even though you stand to make a lot from flipping homes, you need to make accommodations for taxes, which may take a sizeable part of your earnings.

Taxes You Need to Pay as A Home Flipper

For many people, this might be the sad part of flipping. However, you will need to pay taxes on whatever profits you make. If you have been categorized as a dealer by the IRS, the revenue from your flipped property would be taxed using your ordinary income tax rate.

To calculate your profit, you need to subtract all your costs, which include the price of the purchase, from your final sales price. For active investors who earn active profits, the tax bracket falls within 10 to 37 percent (Ivy, 2019).

The IRS states that a dealer in real estate buys a property and sells it to clients in the typical course of their business or trade. Lots of rehabbers are categorized as dealers because they hold on to properties for a short time, and most of their earnings come from flipping properties. Even part-time house flippers may be classified as dealers and would be taxed using ordinary income rates.

In contrast, returns you make from properties you hold for over 12 months are privy to a more beneficial long-term capital gain range of around 0 – 20 percent. An investor can make the choice of occupying the property or renting it out (Ivy, 2019).

Ordinary Income Tax Implications When Flipping Properties

If you are categorized as a dealer, the returns from a flip will be taxed using your dominant ordinary income rate. The range of ordinary income tax rates falls between 10 and 37 percent. Also, the profit is liable to self-employment tax of around 15.3 percent, which is twice the amount you will pay as a W2 employee.

As a dealer, the tax implication on each flip could range from as high as 53.3% to as little as 25.3%, based on your tax bracket. What this means is, you have to bear in mind that all of your profits do not come to you, but rather, a vast part belongs to the IRS (Ivy, 2019).

When is Capital Gains Tax Applicable to House Flipping?

If you are lucky enough not to fall in the dealer category, and you get most of your revenue from purchasing and selling properties after a year, then your taxes will be at the lower capital gains rates on the returns you get from the sale.

If you are serious about going into the business of flipping houses, either as a part-timer or full-timer, then you need to reach out to a professional CPA or accountant who can aid you in structuring your business in a way that would ensure your taxes fall in the lowest bracket possible.

Does Flipping Still Work in Today's Market?

In the past, flipping houses was an ideal chance for an individual with extra funds and an excellent eye for renovation to make money. The market was filled with unoccupied homes from waves of foreclosures caused by the housing crash that blew up some years before. You could purchase a property from a bank, do the needed repairs, put on a coat of fresh paint, and list it for a higher price on the market.

However, with the real estate market heading back to the level it was before the recession, the amount of properties being listed on the market every month is not as high. A day after listing a property, bidding wars begin, which results in homes being sold way beyond the asking price in many circumstances. Buyers who are ready to reside in the homes they buy are finding it difficult to find cheap properties, which implies it is even more difficult for investors in search of homes at low prices.

With these factors in mind, the question many investors tend to ask is: "**_Does flipping still work in today's market?_**"

The answer to this question is *yes*. Flipping is starting to become a recognized business, as an increasing number of organizations like Offerpad, Opendoor and Zillow are providing fast purchases of homes in cash with the aim of fixing and selling for returns. These organizations give more choices to property sellers, but their existence brings about a more competitive market for other investors.

Still, this does not prevent individuals from making an effort to flip properties. However, the requirements for investors who want to attain success are starting to change. In addition to having the capacity to locate the appropriate house and a homeowner who has an interest in selling, you also need the financial ability to get past the stages of renovation and marketing before you can see your returns.

To enhance your possibilities of earning cash from flipping properties, here are a few more steps you can take:

- **Invest differently:** Instead of searching for homes on numerous listing services, try locating those that have not been listed on the market but whose owners are likely to have an interest in a sales offer. You can effectively do this by going through the data of the property and deciding which ones will make a worthwhile investment. Also, accessing property records (which you can get at the office of the local assessor) can offer you information on property taxes and how long the same individual has owned a property. You can also try to buy a property and hold on to it in order to get income from rent. However, all of the management and maintenance tasks associated with that property will fall squarely on you.

- **Begin small**: If you want to go into the business of flipping homes, don't start with a property with lots of plumbing issues and a flawed foundation. You have a better chance of turning in profit with a property that does not require *too* much work, but that can be sold off at an increased price with a few small repairs and competent staging. It will also be less challenging to lure lenders when there is not as much risk involved, particularly if you are going into real estate for the first time.

You won't make an enormous profit at first. However, you won't have bought a money drainer either. The instant you can make sure the house does not have any hidden issues via inspection and you have checked all the legal matters with regard to the property (which we will be discussing further in this book), you can now attract the right buyer by adding a few cosmetic changes.

- **Wait for a downslide in the economy**: This is not a positive strategy when it comes to investing in real estate, but in house flipping, you require a good number of homes listed on the market if you want a great deal on homes to flip. The only method of ensuring a surplus influx of homes is when people are unable to afford to reside in them anymore. And this implies an economic nosedive.

Admittedly, it is more difficult to sell than it previously was, but it is still possible. The key is to locate the sellers available to purchase the right homes at the right price, both of which you can easily do in the market of today. Flipping can still be an effective method of getting high profit, even in the present market. Now that you have armed yourself with the basics, you need to go further by learning the steps involved in the rehab process, which we will break down in the next chapter.

Chapter 2: The

Renovating/Rehab Process

As we covered earlier, rehabbing a property involves the purchase of a cheap or partially deteriorated property, investing your money and time into enhancing it, and then selling it for profit.

Even though this investment is a profitable one, for new investors, it is one of the more expensive and riskier approaches for investing in real estate. A good rehab project requires capital, time, detail, and experience before you can be a pro. So, even though this is an investment strategy with a lot of potential profit, you need to be ready before you go into it. To help with this, we will look into a few steps to take when rehabbing a property.

Appraise the Investment Property

This is a step no real estate investor should ignore before they invest in a property. Get the services of an experienced home inspector, and take a walk around the property you have plans to rehabilitate. This is the most vital step to take if you plan on being successful in rehabbing properties because it will aid you in understanding what you are walking into.

The home inspection will consist of an examination of the property's electrical system, heating, roof, floor, air conditioning system, plumbing, and doors, among other things.

As you can observe, as an investor, you will need the services of an experienced home inspector to finish this step successfully. The investors, aside from being able to point out and give priority to the areas that need repair, can also notice things that you may have overlooked.

Make a Checklist

When you have a clear view of the kind of work the property needs, the next thing you will require is a checklist. You can categorize this as a list of things you need to do to finish a rehab on a property. Here, you need to put down the necessary repairs pointed out by the home inspector and create an estimate of the associated expenses.

This will function as a roadmap that shows you where you need to begin and where you need to head to from there. It will be ideal to begin with the main enhancements needed, and leave minor fixes for last.

Create a Budget

Before you purchase a property to invest in, you need to have an estimate of the cost of repairs. Also, a budget is essential before you begin a rehab project. For this reason, the instant you understand the scope of work required, you need to develop a budget of the amount you are willing to spend on renovating the property.

While doing this, it is crucial to take note of your ROI, as you don't want to overspend on a property and not make any profit. Additionally, remember to estimate the after repair value (ARV), since you aim to make a profit when you are finished with the property. This step is essential in helping you determine if the investment property will increase in value when you are done with the rehab, so you can sell it for a higher value than the price of the purchase, in addition to the cost of renovation.

There is always a chance for unforeseen costs to come up. For this reason, you need to always to make room in your budget for these costs. Lastly, also consider the holding costs when creating your budget, in the event the property does not sell immediately.

Locate The Appropriate Contractor

Many investors choose to save costs by using

inexperienced or cheap contractors. This is not the way to go, as tempting as their lower rates may be, as it usually leads to disaster in the long run. For this reason, it is important to find an experienced and trustworthy contractor with a proper license.

Even though you will spend more, the work will be of more efficient and be of better quality, which helps in adding to the amount of profit you can earn. However, not all contractors come with the same level of skill and experience, so you need to spend a lot of time researching general contractors. Ensure any contractor you choose is insured, licensed, dependable, and suits both your budget and your needs.

Get the Needed Permits

As an investor, you will need some essential permits to rehab a property. It's best to investigate the kinds of permits you need before you purchase a property, so you don't violate the building codes of your area. As a new investor, you can reach out to your local housing department to obtain information on all the necessary permits. Additionally, your contractor can help you decide the permits you have to get based on the kind of work you need to do on the property.

Also, never start a rehab until you have gotten all the necessary permits, as it could result in a loss of your investment. For instance, not having a permit to make upgrades may prevent you from being able to sell. It may also delay projects, cause issues with the housing authority, and drastically elevate your expenses, which can all have a negative impact on your profits. To prevent these things from happening, you need to be smart about your investment and get all the permits you need *before* you begin a rehab.

Rehabbing the Property

Now that you have completed the first stages, you can begin the physical process of rehabilitating the property. The steps below will help you complete a rehab on your investment property:

Begin the Cleanup Phase

The first step is to get rid of all the damaged items and trash like broken windows, doors, and any other detritus around the exterior and interior of the property. The aim of this is to clean up the property and get it ready for the process of rehabilitation, so the project progresses and runs seamlessly. This does not increase the value of the property, but it does not have to cost you anything either, as it is a task you can take on yourself.

Begin with Enhancements to The Interior

According to experts, the interior is the best place to begin. It is the place where people will reside and spend most of their time, so this is where you need to channel most of your investment. If your budget is limited, pay attention to the repairs that will offer you the most returns on your cash. Also, you can use DIY enhancements to spruce up a property's interior, which will help cut expenses.

The first step is to find the core systems in the property that need repairs. Ensure you have hired on plumbers, HVAC contractors, electricians and other professionals to help with these repairs. If you want to complete some aspects like painting on your own, it is certainly possible, but it is better to have a professional painter help out if you can spare the expense.

Lastly, you can move on to the replacement of tiles and flooring. All of these will make the property look more appealing and enhance its value.

Enhance the Exterior

After completion of the interior fixes, you can go ahead with enhancing the exterior to offer it the needed curb appeal. This could range from replacing the front door, shutters, garage door or driveway.

A few ways of enhancing the curb appeal during a property rehab is to improve the landscape, paint the front door, install new lights, mailboxes, and siding. These may seem like minor changes, but they will help increase your property's value and help make sure it feels like home to potential buyers or customers.

Finalizing Stage

Before you consider yourself done with a home rehab project, the last step is to finish up the improvements. You need to go through the changes alongside your contractor and determine if anything requires adjustment. You can also hire a professional to inspect, as they can ensure all the work done is up to standard. Then, you put up the property for rent or sale. But before you can actively engage in the house flipping business, there are a few things you need to put in place, like your financing. We will be taking a detailed look at how you can get funding for your flip in the next chapter.

Chapter 3: Get Your Financing in Place

Investing in real estate can provide you with a consistent stream of income and the opportunity to switch professions. Popular shows on television teaches us that flipping houses is not hard, and you can get the hang of it within a few days.

But the reality is a bit different. You do require the expertise and the ability to make solid plans. However, for many people who invest in real estate or plan to do so, the main challenge they deal with is that of financing. You have to spend cash to make cash. Many investors don't even get to the stage of renovating the property before running out of funds. Then they get stuck with a home they can't sell or continue working on. This is a spot you don't want to find yourself in, and that is why you need to put your financing in place beforehand.

So what available options for finances do you have at your disposal? We will be taking a comprehensive look at these below.

Getting Financing

There are two standard methods of purchasing a home:

- You use your personal cash

- You take out a loan from someone else and pay back after you close

As an investor, your goal should be to attain the level where you will be able to pay for any flip with your own money. However, this is pricey for most first-time investors, so this is not the first option most will have.

If you are going to be taking out a loan from someone else, it is known as "financing" the deal. There are a variety of ways of borrowing cash to finance investment deals, and we will be taking a look at them later on in this chapter.

But first, there are a few things you need to put in place before you apply for loans.

Things to Put in Place Before You Apply for A House Flipping Loan

When investing in real estate, you learn on the go. The more houses you flip, the better you will begin to understand the rights and wrongs when it comes to financing.

However, before you search for financing for house flipping, you need to understand a few things. Knowing these will speed up the process of borrowing and assure your lender that you are good for the loan.

Develop a Business Plan for Every Flip

Lenders typically do not want to loan cash to rehab homes that are not in good condition. However, you have a better perspective of the property than any other individual. It will be your duty to provide the lender with information regarding every home you want to flip.

This is why it is vital to create a business plan for your flip. It does not have to be a very long plan, but you need to put down a comprehensive evaluation of each home consisting of:

- Precise home address

- Investigation of the area where you are purchasing the home

- Sale prices for comparable houses in the area

- Plan, financial forecasts and time needed for the rehab

- Information on any individual who will aid you with the project, e.g., general contractor and partner

- Plan B in the event the renovation does not go how you want

- The present estimate of the property and projected value after repair from an experienced appraiser

- Pointing out each of these areas in your business plan will make lenders take you seriously. It will also make sure you obtain a loan large enough to cover all your expenses.

Get Accurate Estimates of All Costs of Renovation

Many flippers end up not getting enough cash from their lender. If you do not have enough money to settle with your contractors, your project may end up being stuck midway through the renovation. To avoid this issue, your best bet is to develop a broad work scope before you apply for the loan. A scope of work is an elaborate summary of all the costs, timelines, and repairs you will be carrying out in the home.

To put the scope of work in place, you will require assistance from an experienced contractor and appraiser. With their combined efforts, they will investigate comparable projects, and offer you an educated guess of timeline and cost. Before you reach out to a lender, you need to have an elaborate scope of work in place, or you would have no idea of the amount of cash you want to borrow. The scope of work will also consist of two additional numbers that are vital to lenders: the After Repair Value (ARV) and Loan to Value (LTV), which we will be taking a further look at later.

Develop Your Network

One final thing to keep in mind before you apply for your loan is that connections are vital in real estate. Become a part of the (REIA) Real Estate Investors Association or club to connect with other investors. Lots of real estate investors borrow money to finance their projects and also invest in other people's projects. In essence, the individuals you connect with could become lenders or partners in your subsequent deals.

Ways to Get Financing

Having put all these things in place and having determined the amount of money you need, you will now be able to check out your options for financing if you are going with the option of taking out a loan.

Bank Financing

The first place you may want to apply for a loan is at a bank near you. Obtaining loans from banks for flipping is just like getting any other form of mortgage loan. You will define the loan's length and place the down payment required along with any other requirements.

This might sound easy, but getting a loan from the bank to invest in your house flipping business is not without its challenges. To be eligible for the loan, you will need a good credit rating. What's more, if your history in house flipping is not a good one, the bank may not be keen on providing you with financing and could deny the loan.

Personal Loans

A personal loan is a very flexible financing option. When you get a personal loan, you can channel the money to any area you desire, which includes flipping.

To be eligible for this loan, you will likely require a credit score of more than 650. Personal loan charges can be as low as 5 percent, and you will have the capacity to clear it up in monthly installments over three to seven years. The only drawback is that the loan has a cap of $50,000. This may be barely enough for a successful flip, so you may need to merge it with other financing options.

Line of Credit

Tapping into the equity of the home you live in is another well-known option for financing a flip. However, this is only an option if you already own a home. A home equity line of credit (HELOC) or home equity loan (HEL) can offer you funding for your next flip, and you can pull in the cash you require. You will only need to pay interest on the money you utilize. Different from a loan, a line of credit allows you to borrow as high as the limit as required.

The difference between the balance of your mortgage and your home market value is your equity. To be deemed eligible for a line of credit or home equity loan, your home needs to have no less than 20 percent equity, preferably higher depending on the amount you need to borrow. It is also essential for you to have great credit and adequate monthly earnings to pay for both your mortgage and the HELOC or HEL.

Lots of banks will allow you to loan as much as 85 percent of the cost of your residence, after deducting the remainder of your loan balance. The main downside of using the financing method is that your home is being placed as collateral. If you are unable to keep up with the payments, your property can get foreclosed upon by the bank. This can be a potential risk if you plan to use the revenue from your flip to pay for your loan.

Hard Money Loan

A hard money loan is one you get from individuals or investors and not from a bank. Here, the lenders have lower requirements for you to be eligible and offer you the cash for flipping in two weeks or less. Because hard money lenders work alongside borrowers who are not as creditworthy, their rates of interest are higher, usually around 10 to 20 percent. Also, lenders include fees on the loans, which makes the overall cost much higher. This is why it is best to try out other, cheaper, options before you go with a hard money loan.

There are many online platforms and private business loan lenders who focus on providing hard money loans to house flippers. One such platform is LendingHome. There are also other hard money options where numerous investors combine their resources to provide funding for your project called crowdfunding platforms.

Hard money loans aim to keep you "above water" until you are done with renovating your home and selling it. Thus, there is a one-year term attached to the average hard money loan, even though you are open to other longer options. These loans need you to place a little down payment, which is normally around 10 percent. This is because the lender is more concerned about the property's prospects as opposed to the borrower's background.

Hard money loans work differently from other kinds of loans. Here, the lenders provide approval for your loans in segments. First, they offer you the cash for the initial purchase of the home and the initial batches of renovations. The moment the contractor is through with the primary repairs, you will be offered the cash for the subsequent set of improvements, and so on.

Loan from Family and Friends

Under normal circumstances, it is paramount that you don't combine personal relationships with loans or money in general. But, this does not mean it is a bad idea to obtain loans from your friends or loved ones. It is not as tedious as other options of financing, and there is a high possibility that you would get loans at lower interest rates in comparison to banks and hard money lenders. This is because of the personal connection your family and friends share with you.

However, there are a few fundamental rules to borrowing from friends and family. First, you need to put down the terms in writing and specifically state the rate of interest and the time required to pay the loan — a written document aids in protecting both parties. The next rule is to go with the securities laws and IRS laws that apply to family investments.

Look for a Financing Partner

Lots of investors in real estate get stuck in an infuriating situation: They possess a knowledge of the market to know when there is a good opportunity to flip but don't have adequate financing to complete the project. Bringing in a partner, however, can help. They can support you in doing the following:

- Locating the opportunity to flip

- Planning and supervision of the renovation

- Providing financing

Depending on the amount every partner invests, they get a cut in the earnings. Normally, a partner provides the funding for restoration, while the other partner locates the opportunity to flip and supervises the renovation. You may want to stick to the same partner for numerous projects or use a different one for each project.

The share the partner who provides the funds gets is dependent on their negotiation with other partners, and if they are providing support for the project in other ways. The great part of finding a financing partner is that when there is a loss instead of a profit, they also share in the loss. Similar to loans you get from family and friends, you need to put down all the conditions associated with the project using a partnership agreement.

Real Estate Crowdfunding Sites

This is another funding option which is growing more popular in providing financing for all kinds of projects, including flipping houses. The way it works is simple: Lots of people pool their resources together to support real estate projects that pique their interest.

Depending on the site used, most of the crowdfunding sources for house flipping are either developed as equity or debts. Debt funding means that investors purchase an aspect of the loan or the loan itself. Equity crowdfunding, on the other hand, means that investors buy the home being flipped.

401(k) Financing

Taking a loan or withdrawing cash from your 401(k) account is another option to get funding. However, if you are getting close to the age of retirement, this may not be the best bet. But for flippers on the young side, if the rewards are more than the risks, loaning some funds from your 401(k) may be worth it.

Lots of 401(k) accounts provided by employers, give you the chance to take loans of as much as 50 percent of your remaining balance. Self-employed individuals using solo 401(k) plans also have the capacity to get loans of as much as $50,000. This loan also requires you to pay interest, but the cash belongs to you, so the interest and principal you pay back goes to you.

Similar to this, some individuals borrow from their life insurance policy to finance their flip. If you have one, you can ask your insurance company about eligibility requirements.

Your Financial Inventory

Now that you understand the kinds of financing available to you, you need to learn about some essential things to put in place before requesting a loan. Similar to applying for a job that pays well, you will need to be ready when asking people to invest in your business.

Although it is not compulsory for you to put it all down in writing, there are some vital elements of your financial position that you have to prepare in advance. This would be useful during discussions with any individual who wants to fund your investment.

These are the components that normally define the kinds of financing you can get. This means it is crucial for you to take a realistic stock of where you are before you begin to request money from anyone.

The following are aspects of your financial resume your lenders will be concerned about:

Credit Score/Credit History

You need to know your credit score and credit history. If you want to get financing for your projects, good credit is vital. If you have no idea what your credit score is, or you just want to check out your credit history, click here for a free copy. Lots of lenders will begin the process of underwriting by reviewing your credit score. It needs to be over 650 to be great, and if it is not, they may not be too keen on providing you with financing, or if they do, it may be at high interest rates.

This does not imply there are no other options available to you, but by paying attention to developing a good credit score and history, you will have access to the majority of the options for finance available.

Your Earnings

Your income is the next important part of your financial condition. Are you presently doing something to generate consistent income? Do you have a rental property generating money monthly? Lenders will look into all of these sources of income to determine if you will be able to pay back the lines of credit or loans they provide to you.

Your earnings and the longer the time you have had it coming will make lenders more interested in offering you cash. From their point of view, if you have substantial earnings alongside your investment, you will be in a better position to repay loans if the investment does not work out. Similar to credit score, if you have no recurrent earnings, you are still privy to a lot of options even if they are not as much.

Your Resources

Your assets are another vital aspect of your financial condition lenders will take a look at. Providing answers to these questions will be critical:

- Do you have money saved up?

- Do you have landed property or have sufficient equity on your properties?

- Do you have a large retirement fund?

- Do you have other assets you could sell off to settle with lenders in case your investment fails to pay off?

In many situations, lenders will consider loaning you cash if you own assets that you are keen on placing as collateral against the loan. This implies that, if you fail to pay back the loan, the lender takes over the asset instead. For instance, if your home has a decent amount of equity, the lender may request that you place your home as collateral for loans. If you are unable to pay back the loan for any reason, the lender takes over your home.

Debt

Do you presently have any other credit obligations? The truth is, the higher the amount of money you owe, the harder it would be to obtain financing. Sadly, this is something investors in real estate, even those who are already established, must deal with.

There are various kinds of debts, and some are not as bad as others. Any existing liability is going to hamper your ability to pay back extra loans and would reduce the possibility of you getting financing for your flip. Specifically, lenders will check out your income to debt ratio. If your income is way higher than your debts, it means you will be left with more money after each month, and you are more likely to pay back.

Familiarity with Investing

This does not have to do with your finance, but lenders would have an interest in your investment experience. An investor who has had lots of success in investment is more likely to pay back a loan as opposed to one without any experience at all. Having a great business plan can serve as an excellent replacement for experience. Lenders will ignore the absence of experience if you have a clear direction and a detailed plan in place.

As you attain experience, your options for financing will become more copious. But for now, ensure you have at least developed a great business plan, set clear goals, and a means of achieving them. Having determined how you will get your financing, the next thing you have to do is to locate a good agent. This is what we will cover in the next chapter.

Chapter 4: Locate Your Agent(s)

Flipping houses may seem like an easy and fun way to make quick cash on a real estate investment; however, flipping homes is not quite so straightforward in practice. Purchasing, remodeling, and selling a home within a brief time period, while making a profit along the way, is an enormous task even for the most experienced real estate investors.

Fortunately, you don't have to handle this job by yourself. Hiring a real estate agent who is knowledgeable and skilled in flipping homes to help you out can help you save money, time, and hassles during the process.

Collaborating with an agent who is versed in flipping houses can offer you a range of benefits in all phases of the transactions. Agents can aid you in:

- Understanding the conditions of the present market and your local housing market.

- Go through properties and locate the appropriate buyers

- Decide the proper remodeling projects

and find great contractors

- Determine the appropriate list price

Is Your Housing Market Suitable for Flipping Houses?

A local agent with the right experience can aid you in determining whether it is a wise investment for you to flip. Despite popular belief, flipping is not a great idea in all cities. This means, if the conditions of the real estate market in your area are not promising, you won't make a substantial profit on your investment.

And even if your location is not presently the greatest for house flipping, it does not mean things won't change later. The conditions of the real estate market are continuously evolving, due to a range of factors like increasing rates of mortgage and varying rates of inventory. An experienced agent will have the ability to discern the details of your local market.

An Agent Can Locate the Appropriate House for You

House flipping is an uncertain investment that does not provide you with any assurances. You are taking a risk that a home will sell for a higher amount if you spend a certain amount of cash on upgrades and repairs.

So, when making your financial plans, you need to make estimates on the possible value of resale and unforeseen expenses which are typical during a renovation. If you don't get these numbers right, you may not make any profit. Newbies in the flipping business often end up investing too much in a home they want to flip. The higher the amount you pay for the property, the lower the cash available for the remodel. The higher the costs of remodeling and purchasing the home, the lower your profit margins.

Locating the appropriate home to flip is one of the most critical decisions you will make all through the process. Active agents with knowledge of the present market will be knowledgeable in the information you need to aid you in making the right purchase that will let you stay within your budget. Your agent is also your top bet to determine whether the remodel fees will suit your budget or not.

The home's current condition is a core factor in determining which as-is home to buy. It has to have depreciated enough for the seller to receive a bargain, but also be in good enough condition that you can afford to get it fixed. Your agent will also evaluate the surroundings and determine: Are the values of home in your environment declining? Is your home in a growing neighborhood? These are questions agents will investigate before they offer you as-is homes to choose from.

Lastly, an agent can help you figure out the amount of cash you can afford to invest when fixing a home. When making a financial plan, there are a range of numbers you need to consider, which an agent can effectively help you with.

An Agent Offers You Market-Driving Tips When Remodeling

The business of flipping homes comes with a lot of expenses. You can't make renovations like you plan on living in the home or you won't make good returns. You need to answer the following questions:

- Is this going to earn me cash?

- Am I just flushing money down the drain that won't yield me any returns?

The idea is to understand that wise remodeling choices don't mean you need to buy the most expensive materials. When upgrading the kitchen cabinet of your home, you may want to spend huge cash on well-known brand sinks. But when you are flipping a house, going with a brand that is less pricey would also work. You will also be able to save money on these extra expenses.

Agents who have experience in flipping can help you find the best bulk deals to help you save cost. Some agents have direct connections with manufacturers to buy old inventory at a reduced price, or from contractors who have leftover materials from a housing development they have completed.

An Agent Offers You Advise On When-to-Sell

On paper, all houses have a projected value. However, when the moment comes to sell, it is only valued at what the buyer is interested in paying and what the bank is prepared to finance.

An agent who has experience in flipping pays attention to market trends during the process of remodeling to aid their seller in setting the appropriate list price during the right moment. Along with evaluating the value added with the remodel, your agent will consider your expenses to make sure you can get back your investment while making a decent profit as well.

However, there are times when you may be advised by an agent to hold onto the property for some months, or perhaps rent it out for some time, to ensure you have a better chance of earning a higher profit – or ensuring you don't lose cash on the deal. Don't forget that the market conditions of the real estate market are continuously changing and may even change before you finish remodeling.

And if the value of the home falls before you can flip, it may be a good idea to hold on until there is an improvement in the market conditions. When dips like these take place, flippers who do not have a knowledgeable agent by their side can end up selling at a loss.

Newbies to the business of house flipping frequently miscalculate the amount of cash it requires to flip a home, and the level of risk it comes with. However, if you collaborate with a knowledgeable agent, you will be able to make sure that your first flip is a great success.

What Kind of Agent Should You Choose?

The first thing you need to consider is: Are you purchasing or selling a home? Your response here is what will determine the kind of agent you need to work with. Agents who work alongside homeowners who want to sell a home are known as listing agents or seller's agents. These agents act in your interest as a homeowner during the process of listing and negotiation.

Agents who work with individuals who want to buy a home are known as selling agents or buyer's agents. These agents act on behalf of buyers during the process of showing and negotiation. There are a few buyer's agents who work with buyers alone. This means they don't list any houses for sellers whatsoever.

Many individuals in the home selling and buying processes are often confused by the terms selling agent and seller's agent because they sound similar. But, they act on behalf of various parties with unique interests. Selling agents act on behalf of the party purchasing the home, but they only become selling agents after signing of the final contract. On the other hand, seller's agents act on behalf of individuals who want to sell a home. There are also agents who act in the interests of both buyers and sellers. They are called dual agents.

Dual Agents

These agents act on behalf of the seller's and the buyer's interests during the process of purchasing homes. The way it works is simple. Picture yourself going into a home for sale and falling for the location immediately. You know the property is a hot one and won't stay long on the market. You just began to look for a home and have no agent yet. But the listing agent is on the property and is ready to assist you with an offer right at that moment. You don't want to hold off while you find an agent of your own, so you choose to work with him. In this situation, you just got into a functional affiliation with a dual agent.

There is a lot of debate surrounding dual agency because agents will have to remain neutral and work cautiously all throughout the process. After all, they are representing a buyer who wants the least price for a home and a seller who is looking to get the most they can, all for the same home.

Also, in terms of commission, there may be a possible conflict of interest. During a standard sale, the listing agent and buyer's agent share the commission equally. However, dual agents get to keep the entire commission, which implies selling a home for the highest price possible works in their favor. This turns out well for the seller but not so much for the buyer.

Lots of experts in real estate have strong feelings against dual agency, and this is not without good reason. Dual agents are not permitted by law to choose sides in the transaction or share private information. In essence, they get twice the commission while offering less direction and advice to both parties. The majority of the time, only the agent gets any real benefit from this transaction.

Dual agency is not allowed in all states, but it is lawful in some states, like Texas and California. In the states where it is authorized, agents are bound by law to reveal their dual agency before anyone signs a contract. To determine whether or not your state supports dual agency, you need to run a Google search along the lines of: "Is dual agency legal in" along with the name of your state. Having decided the kind of agent you need, the next thing you need to figure out is how to choose that agent.

How to Choose a House Flipping Agent

Choosing the right agent is of critical importance. But what makes a good agent?

There are a few characteristics to look out for which can help you with that. We will be discussing these characteristics below:

Experience

Would you want a surgeon without experience to do a life-saving operation on you? I am guessing the answer is no. The experience a surgeon obtains when practicing their expertise is priceless, and the same applies to real estate agents.

You don't want an agent without any practical experience. You want to look for one who understands how to list and sell homes, the buying process, is familiar with their local market and one who has access to the MLS.

Contrary to popular belief, you don't need someone with specific experience in house flipping. What you do need is someone who comprehends the peaks and valleys of real estate itself. You need to go with an agent whose skill level you are comfortable with – one who understands what they are doing and has solid past experience doing it.

Has Time for You

Believe it or not, when looking for an agent, you don't want to go with the best real estate agent in the district. The agent with their picture on every bench or billboard will not have adequate time to invest in your business. If an agent already has a considerable volume of business and is already deep-rooted in their field, they are more challenging to teach, because they are already used to how they do things. If they have not collaborated with investors before, it can be a difficult task to help them understand your goals from a house flipper's perspective.

Avoid individuals like these and search for agents that are not as popular and established. These kinds of agents will be more eager to collaborate with you and invest the time to learn what you want. They will also be able to provide you with the level of attention you need and deserve.

Devoted to their Job

Focus is essential, and you will want to pick an agent who is focused on what they do and dedicated to ensuring their business works. A flying instructor who works on the side, showing homes, is not the person you want. Look for an agent who is into this as their full-time job, because you will need their complete attention when the process kicks off.

Inspired by Relationships

Many of us work together in business to make money. However, the commission an agent earns should not be the core motivation behind them collaborating with you. When an agent begins giving priority to the commission over the significance of developing a relationship with their partners and clients, then you may no longer be certain your best interest is what they have in mind.

Search for an agent who is inspired by the kinds of relationships they develop with those they work alongside - those who honestly want to aid their customers and work in hand with them to develop a better future. If your agent is helping you look for deals, you have to be sure that their focus is on those deals, and not the commission they will get after the property has been purchased or sold.

Capable of Learning

Similar to locating an individual who has your time, you need to ensure they can learn and are keen on doing so. Any agent who believes he knows everything would not be open to the information you offer them. And because agents don't finish the licensing test with an in-depth knowledge of evaluating properties to flip and calculating ARV, there will be a lot of things you need to share with them.

The agent's capacity to take helpful criticism is key. Those who are open to learning and eager to improve should have the ability to accept it if you tell them they are wrong. They should understand you are not dishing out insults, but are ensuring you both can make more cash at the end of the process. If you would rather represent yourself and save some money in the process, you can do so by getting a real estate license. We will cover how to do this below.

How to Get Your Real Estate License

If you have plans to get your real estate license, you will have to complete the required real estate education in your state. With this kind of education, you will be able to attain some understanding of the financial and legal aspects of real estate dealings. However, you need to note that this information would not be of much practical help for flipping homes.

One of the main benefits of getting a real estate license is being able to access the MLS. It is an unquestionable way to save lots of cash when purchasing homes to invest in. Even if the property is worth $100,000, you can easily save as much as $3,000. With your real estate license, you will have the capacity to list your properties on MLS for free. The MLS has been recognized for selling about 80 percent of sold properties, which is much higher than other kinds of marketing when it comes to house flipping.

The great news is that you will be able to benefit from both ends. You will be able to enjoy the benefits of having a license in real estate without sustaining the additional burden and access to savings. For starters, the moment you have attained your real estate license, agents will be able to legally pay you referral fees when you are flipping homes.

This implies that you can task another licensed agent with doing the work, and have them pay you back a considerable chunk of the commission they get. This offers you more returns and can provide you with extra advance cash when flipping houses. Better still, you can go with the option of hiring virtual assistants who utilize your access to carry out the daily jobs that have to be done when flipping homes. They will have the capacity to do all tasks, including reviewing contracts, uploading listings, and locating properties.

What Can You Use a Real Estate License for?

If you make the choice of getting a real estate license, you will gain access to a field of possibilities. Below are some of the possibilities that come with having a real estate license:

- **Sales Agent**: When you have a real estate license, you will have the ability to aid others in the purchase and sales of properties.

- **Leasing Agent:** Agents also can act as property managers or leasing agents for residential and commercial properties.

- **Broker**: Real estate brokers can manage and license real estate agents of their own.

Is it Compulsory to get a Real Estate License to Flip Homes?

Getting a real estate license for house flipping can be ideal, but only if it benefits you and your business in terms of flipping homes. To go into the business of flipping houses, it is not compulsory to get a real estate license.

Benefits of Having Your Real Estate License as A Rehabber

If you have plans to get your real estate license while in the house flipping business, take a look at some of the benefits you stand to gain:

- **Access to Deals:** With a real estate license, you will have the capacity to access deals you would typically not have known about. Yes, you will be able to access those available on the MLS, but there are also a range of other outlets available. When a new deal is open, you will be one of the first to know; no more waiting for an agent to reach out to you. Sometimes the promptness of execution that comes with having a license is what you need to locate a new deal.

- **New Contacts**: Having a license will expose you to networking events you may not otherwise have been aware of. Real estate is a business that has to do with people and will continue to be. With a license, you will be able to come across people of like mind and locate new deals along the way.

- **Additional Revenue:** With a real estate license, you can earn cash as a real estate agent while investing in real estate yourself. Getting a real estate license is a fantastic way to complement the revenue you are already bringing in from flipping homes. You can channel the subsequent commission you get into your next flip and make so much more.

- **Access to Commissions**: With a license, you will be able to save cash on commissions that usually go to agents in each deal. Real estate commission is often around 2.5 – 3 percent. This means on a purchase of $100,000, you are looking to earn approximately $2,500-$3,000, which would otherwise be paid to your agent. If *you* are the agent on a transaction, this money comes to you, and you can channel it to other areas.

- **Education**: To become licensed, there are certain educational conditions you must meet. However, the industry itself can help you learn a lot. The experience you get from here is adequate to get you through your career in home flipping.

As you can see, there are many benefits to attaining a real estate license. If you are keen on investing the cash and time it takes to get a license, and are prepared to exploit all the benefits that come with being a real estate agent, then it is probably an ideal choice for you. Once you have determined the type of agent you need, or if you have instead decided to get your license, the next step is to decide where to buy your property. The next chapter will take a more in-depth look at this.

Chapter 5: Where You Should Buy?

One of the most vital decisions many newbies in the house flipping business have issues with is where to invest. Investing in the wrong location can result in a massive amount of losses down the road. For this reason, it is essential for you to do thorough investigations before you choose a place to buy.

The buying area of an investor is called their *farm area*, which could be as large as a metro area or as little as one neighborhood. Clearly, the smaller the farm area, the easier it would be for you to know it and the houses within it. However, the bigger the farm area, the more opportunities available to locate incredible deals. How do you determine the right farm area for you?

How to Choose the Right Real Estate Farm Area

Because it can require a considerable amount of time to get high returns from your farm area, the choice you make is critical. Here are a few steps to choosing a profitable farm area for real estate:

Choose a Farm Area Close to Home

If you are just beginning, it may be a great choice to farm your own area. By utilizing a community networking platform, you will be able to position yourself as the real estate expert for the job in a specific area. There are lots of advantages of farming in the area you live which include:

- **You are an Expert in your Location**: By creating your farm area in an environment you already know about and love is the best combination possible. You know the surroundings and many of the inhabitants, and you also have knowledge that would not be easy for non-residents to learn. For instance, you may know a friend of your neighbor who is moving and wants to sell his home soon. In addition to offering fantastic service, you will also be one of the first to know the things happening in the market. A lot of individuals already know you, so it would be less complicated for you to establish business and trust in contrast to a newcomer. Even if you are a new resident in the neighborhood, it is less difficult to make contacts in areas you already reside in. You can prove yourself as a professional in a variety of ways, including hosting local events related to real estate.

- **You Already Have the Contacts**: As someone who resides in an area, there is a possibility that you already have reliable contacts in your farm area. Your friends, family, and people you know are likely close-by. You may already know the owners of local businesses, and you can genuinely recommend the neighborhood to buyers because that is where you live. There are lots of benefits of farming in the area you live in. It is a secure method of drawing in buyers, especially those who are relocating. Consider this for a few seconds: if you just moved to a new area, would you rather collaborate with an agent who resides a few cities away or one who lives or has lived in the area for many years?

- **You Are More Accessible to Customers**: When you reside in the neighborhood you farm, there are prospects to meet potential clients while engaging in your daily activities. Locations like the coffee shop, local gym, hardware stores, and grocery stores all create great opportunities to get new contacts during everyday conversations while engaging in your usual routine. Many times, daily interactions at the mall can transform into great leads. Another reason to keep your farm area close to home is that you will have a better ability to provide previews and showings at the last minute. It is less complicated for you to show potential buyers a fantastic listing that just opened up if it is not far from where you live. It is also less challenging to manage your life and has less impact on your budget. Fees spent on gasoline and vehicle maintenance can be one of the highest expenses for a real estate agent. However, you can drastically reduce these expenses if your farm area is not far from home. In addition to picking a location close to home, it is also vital for you to carry out thorough research on your farm area.

Staying close to home is a brilliant choice; however, you need to do due diligence on your farm area before you make your final decision.

Investigate Your Farm Area

When choosing the appropriate area to farm, doing a thorough investigation is also crucial. Before you begin farming in a particular area, it is ideal for you to get as much information as you can about that area. This will ensure you are confident it is a location you will be glad to work in and offer you the revenue you require to meet your real estate business goals.

In the long run, the demographic elements are one of the aspects you should investigate in the farm area you choose. Below are a few areas to investigate:

- Average age

- Average earnings

- Is it a commuter environment?

- Are there large-scale employers like factories, hospitals, etc.?

- Are there options for transportation?

- Does it have local amenities like nightlife, malls or parks?

- Recent changes

You can get informed about many of these just by running a Google search. However, to attain the age and incomes, you will need to use census data. This data can help direct you to the types of houses people may be looking for, the types of facilities they may have an interest in and the amounts of commission checks you can anticipate. When carrying out your investigation, pay attention to all parts of the neighborhood you respond to personally. For instance, if you are a lover of new developments, it will be less difficult to sell them as opposed to old homes. Because purchasing a house is a decision that is based on emotion as much as finances, buyers are more likely to be responsive to your in-depth knowledge of the subject.

When you select a farm area, you may need to narrow it down to a precise demographic you want to work alongside in that area, which is often called *demographic farming*. For example, you may want to emphasize the houses that have a value of over $2 million. Investigating the local demographics and neighborhood will aid you in choosing an option that is suitable for you. Also, do not forget to consider boundaries when choosing a farm area, as it can help in marketing.

Pick a Farm Area with Clear Boundaries

When you can, make an effort to choose a neighborhood with clearly defined boundaries to aid in marketing your listings. If you have clearly defined limits when farming in real estate, it becomes easier to market your listings. This is because the geographic location you work is defined to others and yourself. Even in large, sprawling areas there are clearly-defined boundaries.

People foresee a specific way of life and home with labeled neighborhoods. Almost every neighborhood in any location has a specific reputation, and exploiting that reputation can aid you in marketing your listings. In addition to boundaries, the size of your farm area is something that must not be overlooked.

Ensure Your Farming Area Is the Appropriate Size

Size is of importance when it comes to geographic farming. You have to make sure the area is vast enough to get reasonable profits, but small enough that you can become an authority without exhausting all your savings. Regardless of where you reside, put the size of your neighborhood into consideration when farming in real estate. The plans you make beforehand will help you save money, time, and make sure you have a significant influx of clients for a long time to come. You could pick the largest farm area you can find, but if the numbers are not right, you will never see success.

Check your Farm Area's Numbers

The moment you locate an environment you want to farm in, the next thing you need to do is run the numbers to ensure the area has adequate sales activity to make your farming profitable. Ideally, you want to pick a farm area with high turnover, sales prices, and low level of competition. However, in reality, it is tough to locate regions like these. To be on the safe side, you may want to search numerous areas and choose the one which is well balanced as regard competition, profit, and price. Check out how to do this below.

- Average Sales Price: It is not as difficult as you may believe to determine the average sales price in your projected farm area, and you only need to take a few steps to do it. First, start up your MLS program and select the area's zip code. You can also use a program like RPR or Realtors Property Resource, as they all provide you with the ability to outline a region on the map.

To determine the average sales price, you need to draw your projected farm area on the map. Next, get all the sold listings for the last two years or more. The average price of the sold houses will be your average sale price. Once you have the average price, you can determine the commission you will get for each transaction. Then, you can decide the number of listings you will need to sell in your farm area to get returns and achieve your set goals.

• Rate of Turnover: To determine this, all you need is to divide the number of houses in your chosen farm area by the number of sold homes in the past two years. Ideally, your chosen farm area should have a reasonably high rate of turnover.

• Competition: After determining that the area has adequate sales activity to keep you going, the next thing you need to get a feel for your competition. Be sure to take note of the leading closing agents for the last two years or more. If you see that a particular agent is already dominating the market in that region, it may be difficult for you to make a move into the market. There would be a major possibility that the agent has been doing work in the area for a long time and is already an authority. On the other hand, if you observe that there are numerous agents making sales in the region, and the turnover is adequate to validate working there, then there is probably a sufficient market for you as well.

Piecing It All Together

Now that you understand everything about the area's demographics, facilities, and types of home available, the numbers regarding turnover, sales activity and competition, you need to combine that information to pick the farm area that is right for you.

When evaluating your farm area for real estate, make decisions using your data. Utilizing a formula to put the numbers together can help you remain confident that pooling your resources in this area won't be a waste of funds. It is unfortunate to get emotionally attached to a region only to discover there is no place for you to develop your flipping business. By doing a good analysis, you can avoid making this costly error in the first place. After choosing a farm area, the next step is to start developing a name for yourself in that location.

How to Develop Authority in Your Farm Area for Real Estate

Here, your objective is to assert yourself as the go-to expert in real estate for the whole community. Let's discuss a few methods of establishing your presence in your chosen farm area:

Direct Mail

This is one of the most efficient and time-tested ways of spreading your message to a precise area. You can take advantage of the EDDM or Every Door Direct Mail service offered by the US Postal Service, which lets you send mailers to every individual in your farm area even if you have no mailing list. If EDDM is new to you, it is a targeted and cost-efficient direct mail service offered by the USPS. It gives you the chance to pick a path for delivering mail through their maps, and then you will have the ability to send your direct mail to each home on that path. The key to remaining in the thoughts of all individuals in your farm area is to reach out to them numerous times. You should be prepared for no less than two mailings before you can expect a response.

Knocking on Doors

If you can handle it, knocking on doors is a fantastic way of familiarizing yourself with homeowners in your chosen farm area. It is free, as all you need is the zeal to create connections with people and some comfortable walking shoes.

One of the great parts about knocking on doors is that you can never tell where the direction of the conversation will go, and in this digital era, it is a way of getting face-to-face with individuals. Lots of people run their advertisements on the internet, and for the right kind of individual, a personal campaign helps you stand apart from the competition.

Door knocking can be a bit daunting, but it is a leading strategy for building authority in a new area. However, if you prefer something less intimidating, door hangers can be an option to look into.

Door Hangers

Using door hangers is another tried and trusted method of reaching owners of homes in your farm area. Door hangers function so well because as opposed to a postcard, which can get mixed up and abandoned in the mail, homeowners need to take off the door hanger physically before heading into their home.

Facebook Advertising

Facebook is an efficient advertising platform for those who are focused on real estate. With Facebook, you can target using zip codes and a range of other benchmarks like income, recent job, and interests, among others.

There is an excellent volume of data available for you on Facebook to capitalize on and locate your target audience. There is a "ready to move" category which consists of individuals whose online conduct is consistent with those who are ready to relocate. You can take advantage of this to find the right clients in your farm area.

Take Part in Online Local Forums

Taking part in online forums devoted to your chosen farm area is another ideal method of developing trust there. Sometimes, the best way to build trust is to take part as a regular citizen who also works as a real estate agent.

Look for the platforms your farm area have online gatherings and become a part of the conversation. Search for neighborhood subreddits, Patch sites, city data forums, and Facebook groups. Make contributions to the discussion and drop in a listing frequently, and keep in mind that anytime you relate with others, you are representing your business too.

Meetup Groups and Local Events

Local events and Meetup groups are arguably some of the best methods of creating connections to individuals in your farm area. Give priority to being social and let business come next. Help raise funds for your local rescue organization or a new pool in the community.

Genuinely take part in the area you love, and the rewards will come in droves. The moment they know who you are, they will find you in search of the services you render. Take pictures you love and post them on your online platforms, and use those moments you connect with the community to show your genuine self. Search for events you will enjoy taking part in like charity events, fairs, sales, or anywhere else the community assembles.

Get Your Website Ranked on Google Using Local Search Terms

If you are new to the business of flipping houses or real estate in general, you will undoubtedly need a website. Agents without any online presence are losing out on business and relevance as society becomes more digital, so make sure you position yourself where clients are looking.

Google is a great tool to aid you in remaining in the minds of people in your farm area. For instance, assuming your farm area is Wicker Park in Chicago. If you incorporate the words "Wicker Park" in the URL of your website, you will show up on more Google searches for the neighborhood. Something like "Wickerparkhomes.com" will draw you nearer to the first page of search results.

Real estate farming is a tested means of becoming an expert in your location and closing more sales. If you invest the time to do comprehensive research on your farm area before you spend any money, it will ensure you reap lots of rewards down the road. While at the start, this may seem like a huge task to carry out, but the tips we discussed in this chapter can help you become the go-to real estate expert in your farm area. Having figured out a suitable farm area for your real estate transactions, the next step is to decide who you should buy from. We will learn this in the next chapter.

Chapter 6: Who Should You Buy From?

Who you buy real estate from is as vital as all the other aspects of house flipping we have covered thus far. In this chapter, we will be taking a look at some of the best strategies you can use for investment in real estate. There are typically five kinds of scenarios you should focus on when investing.

They include:

- Owners with equity

- Absentee owners with equity

- Owners without equity

- Bank-owned foreclosures

- Properties at auction

Buying from Owners with Equity

Sometimes, homeowners deal with personal issues which may compel them to let go of their properties at a reduced rate. Some of the major reasons for this include financial distress, death, relocation, and divorce.

It may be hard to purchase from sellers dealing with financial problems because the mortgage they owe could be way beyond the worth of their property. This means they are unable to sell at a reasonable price and afford to pay off their mortgage simultaneously.

However, in other situations, the homeowners are in haste to sell and don't owe so much on their mortgage, which means they can sell to you at a reasonably decent price and still pay off their mortgage – they have equity in their home. When a homeowner in distress has equity on their property, it means there is an amazing chance for you to come in and aid the homeowner out of this issue while ensuring you get a great deal which will make you profit down the road. Here, everyone wins.

Buying from Absentee Owners with Equity

When you come across the phrase "absentee owners," it usually refers to landlords. In a few situations, these are homeowners who have become landlords due to circumstance. For some, they inherited a home which they had issues selling off and rented it out for the time being. Others may have relocated to another geographic area.

In other situations, these are investors who bought the property for the sole purpose of making money from it through rent. All of these scenarios can offer you profitable deals.

Buying from Owners Without Equity

Many investors or homeowners who are dealing with issues on their property may go with a short sale. A short sale is a unique form of purchase straight from the owner of a home whose debt on his loan is higher than the value of this property and is having a hard time meeting their mortgage payment. The process of a short sale begins when the owner of the home, who is having issues making their mortgage payment, authorizes their lender (which could be the bank or other lenders) to sell their home at a value below the amount they owe as a mortgage.

Most times, the bank would instead choose to go with a short sale than a foreclosure because the process of foreclosure does not come cheap. Lots of money and time is invested into it, and the bank may end up selling for much less than they got from the short sale. In the end, the short sale is a win for all parties involved.

Buying Foreclosures at Auction

If you are an experienced investor, this could provide you access to lots of great deals, but as a new investor, it might not be a great option. The reason is, you need to invest a lot of time into your due diligence, and skipping even a small aspect of it could lead to severe financial losses down the road.

When you purchase a property using this method, all the liens, claims, and debts associated with the property become yours. However, this does not mean you can't find great deals via auctions.

Buying (REO) Bank-Owned Foreclosures

REO properties are those have passed through the process of foreclosure, and nobody was interested in buying at the auction, and now, the bank is going through a typical sales process in real estate, in a bid to dispose of the property. A licensed real estate agent helps in listing the property on the MLS, and people who are interested in buying turn in their offers the same way they would at other properties.

The asset manager, whose role is to supervise the sale of the REO properties, will review the offers. They have the power to reject or accept offers made on the property. If the asset manager accepts an offer, a leading official in the bank makes the final approval. After approval of a sale, and contracts have been signed, the property goes through the usual closing process which takes around 3-6 weeks to complete.

Choosing the Best Option for You

When determining the situations and sellers that will be ideal for you, consider the following:

- **Your disposition**. Are you the kind of person who loves talking to people? Are you understanding enough to place yourself in the trying shoes of the sellers? If yes, it could be a great choice to work with owners. If this is not the case, you may want to go with other options where the sellers are corporations and not homeowners. When choosing a seller to do business with, it is vital to consider your personality and how it could affect your business.

- **What is your timescale?** Do you want a project that could span a few months before you close or one that you can close fast? If time is not vital to you, then you can go for a short sale or REO. If you want something quicker, you can purchase a property at an auction. Your timescales also play a major role in helping you choose a seller.

- **Where you are situated**? Do you reside in a location that has numerous homeowners with equity? If yes, aiming at homeowners in distress or reluctant landlords can bring you fantastic leads. Are there plenty of short sale deals and REO on your MLS? If yes, this may be an avenue to exploit. The area you are located in and its present real estate market will have huge roles to play when targeting sellers.

After you figure out who you will buy from and which seller is best for you, the next thing you have to do is learn how you can find the best deals, which we will explore in the following chapter.

Chapter 7: How to Locate

the Best Deals

At this point, you understand your financing options, and you know how to find your agent. Also, you already know where to buy and who to buy from. But how do you find the properties that suit your requirements? You can go about it via numerous ways which we will be discussing in this chapter.

Use the MLS

The MLS (Multiple Listing Service) is a databank assembled by real estate brokers. It lists all the properties for sale in a geographical location, together with the properties' features and other essential information. The MLS can only be assessed by licensed real estate agents. As previously discussed, this is one of the major benefits you stand to gain if you get licensed. However, if you have not been licensed, another great way of gaining access is to collaborate with a licensed agent. This could take the form of a favor, business partner, or team member. If you are hiring a real estate agent for your project, make sure they can access the MLS.

Taking advantage of the MLS to locate good flip deals offers some benefits in making the right home purchase. For one, the majority of the properties to be sold in a location are listed in one area. Additionally, the listings tend to come alongside other useful information as compared with what you can find on other platforms. If you want to purchase a property to flip and you have no way to access the MLS, there are other platforms you could try out. Sites like Realtor.com and Zillow.com offer you comprehensive information on properties for sale in a given location. However, the information may not be as in-depth as what you can find on the MLS listings.

Become a Part of a Real Estate Investment Group

During the past few years, real estate investment groups have become more recognized. There is a chance you have a few around you, and it may be an excellent idea to try them out. These groups can provide you education and networking prospects that may be significant when in search of a property to flip. Additionally, these groups usually show real estate listings on their sites and in their newsletters.

You can find a lot of these groups on social media platforms like Facebook and LinkedIn. A lot of these groups offer you assess to meetups and conferences, which will provide you the chance to meet with prospective sellers of properties and investors in person.

Search for Auctions

Auctions are great places for you to check if you have cash available to purchase the home. There are a lot of places you can look at for great properties such as a sheriff's sale, estate auction or private auction. Many regions list the properties for foreclosure numerous weeks before the sale takes place. Estate auctions and private auctions are also typically publicized weeks ahead of time. By going through these lists, you have the opportunity to look at a property before its sale date. However, you can only check out the property from far off and won't be able to go closer for a more detailed look.

However, there is a chance of becoming too involved with the bidding when purchasing properties at a live auction. Many bidders do not remember their plans before the auction and fall into the trap of bidding higher than they originally budgeted for. If you are in a bidding war with other buyers for a property, create a limit for yourself and follow it.

Purchasing through an auction also comes with another hazard. Many auctioneers will ask that you pay a fee in advance before you win a bid. This fee is usually 10 percent of the property's purchase price. It will also be mandatory for you to complete the payment within 30 days of the auction date. If you fail to complete the payment, you will have to let go of the deposit. As a result, this method is not ideal for those who don't like risks. If you want a less risky option, you can try speaking to a wholesaler.

Talk to Wholesalers

Wholesalers deal in locating properties for rehab, placing them under contract and then finding a buyer who will perform the house flip. The buyer replaces the wholesaler in the contract and pays the fee to the wholesaler for being the intermediary.

Although this is not the most budget-friendly method of finding deals, it will ensure you save time and money going forward. Many wholesalers are very engaged in what they do and have lots of connections in specific areas.

Use Classifieds

The use of daily newspapers for the sale of properties was once popular. Unfortunately, this is no longer the case as recognition of print media keeps dwindling with the rise of technology and the convenience that comes along with it. Many newspapers still run classified ads, but for many investors, this is not on the top of their list.

This is not without good reason. It can be hectic to search through ads listed in a newspaper. You also do not have the capacity to search using a specific category or feature and the downsides outweigh the benefits. If you want something convenient, and less tasking, using an agent would be a better option.

Find an Agent

If you don't know an area too well, you can add an agent to your team. Hiring an agent is an efficient way of getting a rehab property. Agents will have insight into the best locations for flipping, and this offers them the ability to screen the opportunities available to you. They will also have the ability to offer you supplementary advice on investing for your house flip.

Getting the services of an agent who focuses on REO can also be an effective method of finding great deals. REO stands for "real estate owned," and refers to properties claimed by lenders when owners are unable to make their loan payments. A lot of these homes will have already had a foreclosure process, and possibly an eviction process.

Also, the past owners of the homes may not have invested in caring for and maintaining the property while the foreclosure was ongoing. As a result, you can get these properties way beyond the market value, which is why they are ideal for flipping. Lots of lenders have connections with a few real estate agents that deal in selling these types of properties. Locating them is easy, as all you need to do is collaborate with an agent who has access to new homes available for rehab on the market.

Use a Short Sale

When homeowners are unable to pay their mortgages, they may be offered the opportunity of selling the home "short" by the bank. This means the owner sells the home for less than the value they owe on the mortgage. Many banks prefer this option to foreclosure because of how pricey and consuming it is to sell properties that have been foreclosed upon. Short sales could create an excellent opening for you as a buyer to purchase properties from homeowners who want to let go of the property quickly.

Buying a property via a short sale also comes with its downsides. For one, it takes a larger amount of time to finish the transaction, as opposed to a typical sale. The reason is because the short sale, and its price, require the lender's approval. What's more, lenders who agree to this hardly ever pay for any extra fees that a typical seller usually makes. What this means is that you could be faced with additional closing costs. You can speak to a real estate agent to find out more about short sale listings.

Use REO

When a home gets foreclosed in an auction, the bank or lender will become the new owner. These properties are classified as real estate owned listings or REO. Many banks are happy to let go of REO properties to clear up their accounts, and this means you are probably going to find it at a lower price. Some lenders send listings for REO properties through emails or newsletters. But, you can contact your local banks to find out if they have properties to dispose of. However, before you buy, be cautious of severe property damage and liens before making the purchase.

Seller Direct

When the cost of properties are at their peak and the market is buoyant, it may not be easy to find flipping deals. Sometimes, you may be unable to pinpoint these deals because the seller has not yet made the decision to sell their property. Seller direct means getting across to homeowners at strategic moments, like the period before they list their properties, and make them an irresistible offer on their home before it hits the market. There are a lot of tools that use public data to outline tendency-to-sell models. If you want a more conventional option, taking a drive around can be what you need.

Take a Drive Around

Driving around is an orthodox way of finding flipping deals. All you need to do is step into your vehicle and drive around your target area. Look out for properties that seem distressed, like those with heaps of mail and newspapers, yards filled with overgrown brush, and boarded windows.

If you find a property like this, take down the address and do some investigations of your own to find the owner or seller. This will help you make an offer, and you may end up with a profitable deal.

Check The Internet for Listings

You can locate numerous lists on the internet that show foreclosures, short sales, and distressed properties. Based on the type of list, they may be grouped by city, zip code, or town. These lists are fantastic locations to check when looking for a great flip deal.

You can access many of these lists without a fee, while others may require payment. It's best to start with a free listing as you may find the deal you are after here. There are also a lot of websites available for you to use, like   BankForeclosedListings.com   and BankForeclosureSale.com.

The above are some of the great ways to find the best investment deals. However, if you fail to familiarize yourself with the essential formula for a flip, you may end up buying properties that won't offer you any revenue. Worse still, you may end up purchasing an overpriced property.

So what is the flipping formula? The next chapter will help you gain a better understanding.

Chapter 8: What is the Financial Formula for Flipping Homes?

When it comes to flipping properties, knowing the numbers is of utmost importance. If you want to make the most profit from a flip, you need to know the formula for flipping houses.

In this chapter, we will take a look at some of the essential formulas you need to learn to be successful in this business.

ARV or After Repair Value Formula

The ARV is an approximation of the future value of a home or property after repairs have taken place. It is a property's value after you have made your upgrades.

Numerous factors can affect how you calculate your ARV. The two core areas, though, are the purchase price of the property and the value of repairs.

The formula for calculating ARV is: (Renovation Cost) + (Property Purchase Price)

70% Rule Formula

If you are experienced in flipping homes, you have probably come across the formula known as the 70 percent rule. You take a home's after repair value and multiply it by 70 percent. Then you deduct the repair cost, and the remainder is what you need to purchase a property if you want to make a significant profit.

The formula for this rule is: (ARV x 70%) – Repair Cost.

When Can You Go Against The 70% Rule?

If you are not an expert at flipping, it is not advisable to go against this rule. However, if you are in a market that is highly competitive and you need to offer higher than 70% to clinch the deal, then do so. There are costly cities like Los Angeles with intense competition, where you may be unable to win a bid at 70% without rehab. In areas like this, you might need to adjust your numbers.

Maximum Buying Price

You need this formula to do an in-depth analysis of the total costs in the project after you have used the 70 percent rule to determine how valuable a property is.

To calculate this, use the formula: ARV - Costs of Repair - Funding Costs - Selling Costs.

Expected Return on Investment

This is the value you anticipate to make once a home has been sold. The higher your ROI (return on investment), the higher your profit. This is what all investors strive for. If your ROI is low, your profit will be too. Your budget, ARV, and timelines will affect your ROI.

To determine the expected ROI, use this formula: Net Profit/Total Investment x 100.

The Formula for Offer Price

The offer price is the amount you are willing to pay on a home. Here, you need to be careful, so you don't pay too much for a property. You want to drop an offer price that is beneficial to you and not too low for the seller.

To determine the offer price, use this formula:

ARV - (Renovation Cost + Holding and Closing Costs + Cost of Financing + Profit Target) = Offer price.

After learning the flipping formula and making the calculations for your next flip, now is the time to make an offer on a home.

Chapter 9: How to Make Offers

Placing an offer to buy a home is a major step, and it can be very unnerving, particularly as it's probably going to be a transaction that requires a lot of cash. You need to ensure the process is as smooth as it can be.

Here, we will take a look at a few tips to help you go through the course of submitting an offer and engaging in negotiations to ensure you have a more seamless transaction.

Crafting a Good Offer

When making an offer on a home, you don't want to make just any offer. It has to be a good offer if you're going to stand a chance of winning the bid. Here are a few essential tips to note when making an offer.

Run a Comparative Market Analysis (CMA)

Before you turn in an offer, request that your real estate agent run a CMA for you. It offers you a current image of your local market, which is vital if the property has been on the market for a while. It also points out a property that is priced beyond its value. For instance, if the CMA proposes a market value in the range of $150,000 - $180,000, and the home is valued at $210,000, you will have the opportunity to negotiate. Your CMA can also offer you a realistic point to begin your initial offer.

Consider Market Indicators

Outside the outcome of a CMA, how long a property has been on the market is an excellent sign of buyer interest. You can find this date in the MLS and other websites for listing homes. Knowing the average time homes in your area spend on the market will provide you with an understanding of the general state of the housing market in that area. It will tell you if it is a seller's market, buyer's market, or none. In the seller's market, homes sell quicker, while in the buyer's market, homes stay on the market longer.

Any offer you make has to show the present local demand and should align with the other offers that may be provided to the seller. For example, a seller whose property has stayed on the market for a long time and battled to draw in bids would be keen on accepting a lower offer as opposed to one who just listed the home. In hot markets, properties may remain on the market for a few hours or days and draw in bids at the list price or above it.

Sill, every situation differs. For example, even in the most competitive seller's market, newer homes that are overpriced and older properties with severe issues battle still can draw in decent offers. When you are uncertain, ask your real estate agent for direction. The same applies if *you* are representing your interests – ask someone who understands the local market for guidance. Even if you know the temperature of the market, you may not have an edge if you don't find out the seller's motivation.

Determine The Motivation of the Seller

The reason behind a seller letting go of his property is just as important to know as the overall temperature of the market. Some sellers need to dispose of their properties fast as we have covered earlier. This may be as a result of financial constraint, relocation, or an urgent desire to amass capital to buy another property. These sellers are called motivated sellers and will often be eager to accept much lower than their asking price, mainly in the buyer's market.

On the other hand, there are sellers who are not in a hurry to sell a property, such as those who inherited a property they don't need. These sellers have no problem waiting for the relevant offers. Watch out for signals, based on what the seller says, to determine the group your seller falls into. In addition to this, it can also be helpful to learn about competing offers.

Learn About Other Offers on the Home

In a lot of jurisdictions, it is not mandatory for sellers to reveal the purchase offers they are considering. It only goes into public record when the seller agrees to an offer. But if you have an experienced real estate agent on your team, they may be able to learn about the other offers you are contending with. Before you tender your offer, ask your agent to find out about showing activity that took place recently from the seller's agent. The agent of the seller may not tell your agent if the seller is considering another offer but may admit if there has been a lot of interest in the property. If you are representing yourself, the responsibility of doing this falls on you.

If you have a hunch that the seller has various offers available, waste no time in submitting your offer, and ensuring the offer is as seller-friendly as it can be. This means a higher offer price and fewer costs paid by the seller. If you suspect that the seller does not have many offers on the property, submit a more buyer-friendly offer, as you will probably have the chance to negotiate.

Get a Pre-Approval Letter if it Is a Financed Deal

If you are getting financing, request that your lender provides you with a letter of pre-approval. This letter will show that you have provisional approval for a mortgage loan up to a specific amount. To get this letter, you may have to schedule a meeting with a loan officer, agree to a credit check, and make asset and income verification information available.

This is different from a final loan approval, as pre-approval enhances the certainty that your application for a loan will eventually be approved. Because of the slim possibility of final approval, lots of sellers don't take financed offers seriously if there are no pre-approval documents attached to it. If the transaction is in cash, pre-approval is not needed as it does not involve any financing.

Make A Larger Down Payment

The more cash that comes with your offer, the more appealing it will look to the seller. The reason for this is that smaller loans have a lower possibility of failure due to an issue with financing.

Get an Attorney to Analyze the Offer

Purchase offers for real estate are one of the vital

legal documents you will need to sign. Even if it is not required by the laws of your state that a licensed attorney be present to create purchase offers, it can be a massive benefit to you to get an attorney to analyze your offer and make sure you are not walking into a trap.

Engaging in Negotiations

Before you go into the process of negotiation or sealed bidding, you need to determine the amount you want to spend and think critically before you go beyond that amount. You need to remember that there are extra costs that come with purchasing a property.

Best Bidding Strategies

The best bidding tactic is dependent on the process of bidding – if they are the typical open negotiations or sealed bids. We will be taking a look into each below:

Open negotiations

Start your bid low

Similar to any other form of negotiation, you need to begin low. A good idea would be to make your offer 5 – 10 percent less than the seller's asking price. Remember that many sellers consider this and list their homes for higher than they would accept or anticipate.

Typically, the agent will inform you of any bids that

are higher than yours and offer you the opportunity for a second or sometimes third bid. You should only make an offer higher than the asking price if you are aware the seller has already gotten a similar offer, and you believe there are numerous other buyers.

Stay Calm

Remain calm and polite always. If you get frustrated, you will only push people off.

Play Hard to Get

Play hard to get; however, remember to be realistic. If you believe you are dealing with a desperate seller, it may not suit you to seem too interested.

Reach Out to Sellers Directly

It may be helpful to directly reach out to the seller and make your negotiations in person. But note that they could be more challenging to negotiate with as opposed to the agent whose aim is to close the deal fast.

Lastly, don't let the other things that come with the deal be your primary motivators. For instance, used white appliances, except when very new, are not usually worth much, and it is easier to convey them with the home than move them.

Sealed Bids

If you are making a bid through sealed bids, you will need to put down your offer in an envelope and literally seal it. Then, the agent will offer all the bids to the seller, who will typically accept the highest. The aim of this is to get the highest price, because buyers who are worried about someone outbidding them, will put in their best offers. Most times, the seller gets higher than their asking price in a sealed bid.

In some locations that have extremely high demands, sealed bids have become the standard. It can be tedious to dig through sealed bids. Although it may be very enticing to offer an amount way beyond your set budget to win the bid, it is essential you keep to your budget.

If in the end, if you bid higher than the asking price, you may not be covered by your mortgage company. So you need to ensure you have the financing required before you make a bid.

Holding Deposits

Some sellers demand that a buyer provides a little bit of money alongside their offer. It is known as a holding deposit. It is to prove that they see the offer as important enough to invest their money.

Not every seller requests a holding deposit. The ones who request for it are in very hot markets.

There are numerous kinds of holding deposits such as:

- Refundable deposits irrespective of the party that backs out

- Non-refundable deposits if you, the buyer, walks away. However, there will not be a refund if the buyer walks away. This gets rid of buyers who have no plans of buying the property.

- Non-refundable deposits. These should be avoided because it implies that the seller can sell to another individual and you will only be able to get your cash back if you take them to court.

Holding deposits are not encouraged by many real estate agents. There are a few who don't support them at all because they make the deal take pointlessly longer. Lastly, never offer a holding deposit to the seller directly. The solicitor of the seller usually places the deposit into an escrow account. After submitting your bids, you need to be ready for the possible counteroffers from sellers.

Seller Counteroffers and Responses

The moment you turn in your purchase offer, the seller will need to respond when the consideration window ends. If the seller has a lot of offers on the property, and your offer is not one of the most appealing, the seller may disregard the offer.

The most common ways sellers respond to purchase offers are by:

Agreeing to The Terms

When the seller is fine with the offer, they accept it and signs a written agreement, which then establishes a binding purchase agreement. Making adjustments is still possible up until the closing date, so long as both parties are in agreement and have signed a contract.

Rejecting/Refusing The Terms

If the terms of the offer do not favor the seller, the seller can reject the offer. Although dealing with rejection is painful, the significant part is that the seller is willing to interact with you. This means you can follow up on the rejection with an offer that is more seller-friendly.

Make a Counteroffer

When the offer is appealing, but not wholly satisfactory, the seller can alter it by making changes to core aspects like the price of purchase and seller-paid expenses. Then they sign it and send it back to you, the buyer. This is called a counteroffer. You can decide to agree with the counteroffer in writing, or further alter it, sign it and send it to the seller once more to analyze. This process can last for as long as needed until the seller agrees with the offer or one party stops negotiations.

In a few situations, sellers who get many offers at the same time, individually negotiate with every buyer to get the best deal they can. If the seller needs to reach a binding agreement quickly, they may request that each buyer who has an interest provides their best offer possible, and go with the best one.

After you make an offer on a property, the next step will be to do your due diligence before you finally close the deal.

Chapter 10: Doing Your

Due Diligence

Due diligence is the act of conducting research before you buy a property. The kind of home you want to buy is not vital, but if you're going to reduce all of the risks, then you need to do a few things. Ensure you do an inspection of the property and an appraisal, as those are some things you require for due diligence.

It does not have to stop here. If you are purchasing a property, you can do an investigation of your own. In this chapter, we will be covering all that has to do with due diligence. It also consists of due diligence tips, which will ensure any house flipping transaction is a success.

The Legal Due Diligence

It is not possible to determine everything about a property at a glance. For this reason, you have to consider the title, deeds, and zoning, and other factors.

Due Diligence Tasks

Due diligence aims to find out whether all your projections in the initial analysis of the project are correct or wrong. In essence, you will be using this time to make sure you have all the needed numbers to go forward with the project or not.

If you have gotten to this point, you should already be through with the majority of your due diligence tasks. However, it may not be as comprehensive as you need it to be. With this knowledge, here are a few things to do when finishing the purchase:

Do Your Homework

Take a walk around the property. Check out any documents before you sign, calculate the cost of insurance and other expenses, take a look at trends in the environment and other market values.

You need to do all you can to make sure the property you are buying will bring in good returns. Be detailed as you weigh the benefits and drawbacks of your prospective investment. When it comes to due diligence, there is no detail too minute.

Be prepared for an appraisal, if financing. An appraisal defines the property's value. If you have plans to take out a mortgage, lenders will need you to perform an appraisal to make sure the property is worth its value. After an assessment, if the property is not worth its value, you will not get an approval for the loan except if the seller reduces the cost to what the property is determined to be worth.

A home inspector and an appraiser will help in inspecting the property. However, the appraiser deliberates on things like location, size of property, upgrades, and other conditions. Then the appraiser will compare it to other properties in the area similar to what you want to buy in the area. When you do an appraisal, sellers will be unable to increase the prices without value.

Go Through the Title History

Carrying out a title search before you go on with the final purchase process of a property is vital to ensure you will get the title clear and free of any ownership issues. If the past owner has previously done some work on the property and has failed to make complete payment of the full amount to the contractor, the property may come with a lien attached that needs to be paid before they can sell the property. If the buyer has no information about this lien, it could lead to them paying for the pending amount before they can release the title clear and free in your name.

After carrying out a title search, it is essential that you get owner's title insurance to save you from challenges that may not have been revealed when searching the title. These kinds of problems can include:

- Forgery

- Undisclosed heirs

- Deeds omissions

- Recording mistakes etc.

The owner's title insurance safeguards you from unidentified liens on the property that may come up after you close. Insurance companies have a responsibility to clear these up.

Take a Look at Homeowners Association *Restrictions and Covenants*

If you are purchasing an apartment, condo, single-family home, or townhouse in specific areas, be prepared to follow HOA requirements. HOAs often come with strict covenants and regulations that owners must adhere to. These contracts are put in place and enforced to safeguard the neighborhood's values and appearance.

For example, there may be a limitation or restriction to the color you can paint the exterior of your property. The same could also apply to parking an RV on the street or driveway. If you go against any of these rules, you may be liable to pay fines to the HOA. You need to go through the restrictions and covenants of the HOA before you purchase any property.

Inspect The Property

You need to inspect your property. The inspection will be one of your final chances to ensure you are purchasing a sound property.

You will want to hire a licensed home inspector to help with the inspection instead of doing it on your own. However, you need to note that home inspectors are not perfect and can miss issues. Home inspectors only take note of things that you have to replace or repair. This information is significant, but it is not *all* the data you need to make a calculated decision. Here are some other areas you will want to cover:

- Find out if the property has a lot of radon. It is known to cause cancer.

- Ensure there is no mold in the home.

- If there is a well instead of public water, you need to check the water quantity and quality.

- If the house was developed before 1978, you might want to find out if there is lead paint. This is vital if you have kids below the age of six.

Preparing for The Inspection of a Property

It is necessary for you to get ready for the inspection of the property by noting down parts of the home you want the inspector to check before they show up. Your checklist should consist of:

- Foundation

- Exterior paint

- Appliances

- Driveways and walkways

- Attic space

- Roof

- Downspouts and rain gutters

- Power outlets, electrical panel, and light switches

- Floors, ceilings, and walls

- Windows and doors

- HVAC system, heating, cooling and thermostats

- Water heater, plumbing fixtures, and faucets

- Garage

- Basement

- Balconies and Porches

- Railings, steps, and stairs

A proper inspection should last for a few hours. Ensure you are physically present so you can learn as much as you can about the condition of the property. Put down notes of your own, take pictures, and ask questions.

What a Home Inspection May Not Entail

Although an inspection scope may differ, the primary concern of inspectors are the physical aspects of the home. This may cover a lot of things, but it may not cover everything. Some things that may be ignored which you will need to check out yourself include:

- Landscaping and trees

- Sewer lines

- Lawn sprinklers

- Odors

- Drainage

- Internet and cell service

- Chimney and fireplace

- Swimming pool equipment

- Rats, mice, and other rodents

- Wood-destroying pests like carpenter ants and termites

- Floors hidden by carpeting

There are numerous kinds of inspections you need to perform on a property you want to invest in. We will be taking a look at some of the types of checks you can carry out and why it would be beneficial to spend some of your funds to get specific inspections done before you make a purchase.

Note that it is beneficial to be physically present during the inspection, as this will help you better understand the property's condition and offers the chance to ask any questions that may come up.

General Home Inspection

Before you go ahead with the purchase process of a home, you need to perform a general inspection. The majority of lenders require this inspection if you are getting a loan. Typically, a licensed contractor or home inspector with the right certifications will examine everything in the home. This consists of a complete report on the situation of cooling, roof, electrical, water heater, kitchen appliances, and heating. The inspector will offer you an elaborate report on any problems they find and how serious those problems may be.

After the general inspection, it is not unusual to find out that there are necessary repairs you need to do, which might bring about possible expenses and dangers. There are times when the costs for these essential repairs will be high enough to result in the buyer canceling an offer and continue their search for a property with less risk. Ensure the language in your purchase agreement includes conditions that let you cancel your offer after an inspection. It should also protect you from losing any cash you have put in as a down payment.

(WDO) Wood-Destroying Organisms *Inspection*

Many lenders also ask you to do a WDO inspection of a property. This inspection allows you to determine if there is any wood rot in a property's structure. Water damage or termites can lead to wood rot and inspectors will check the interior walls, garage and exterior sliding for this kind of damage.

Deep wood rot can depreciate the structural integrity of a property. In the report presented to you, the inspector will let you know the severity of the wood rot or how minor it is. This will provide you with extra information to aid you in determining if the risks are more than the returns.

Lead-Based Paint Inspection

This is an inspection required by law for homes developed earlier than 1978. If the seller knows that there is a presence of lead-based paint in the exterior or interior of the house, they are legally bonded to convey this information to prospective buyers.

You, as the buyer, also need to carry out your tests own for lead-based paint as part of your due diligence. This form of paint is dangerous to the health and will cost money to get rid of before you or anyone else can live in the property.

Radon Gas Inspection

Inspection for radon gas is not as common as the other aforementioned inspection types. However, this gas can be found in houses all around the United States.

The Surgeon General and EPA also states that being exposed to this gas for long periods has been proven to contribute to numerous deaths related to lung cancer each year.

Once the inspections are complete, you will be left with the following options:

- Going ahead with the sale after accepting the condition

- Walking away from the deal

- Renegotiating for a more suitable deal

If everything seems sound, go ahead and sign a document that informs the seller that you agree with the conditions.

However, if there are serious problems with the property, what do you do? In a situation like this, you can first renegotiate the deal before you walk away. For instance, if you notice faulty plumbing and there needs to be a complete change in the plumbing, don't take off yet; you can request that the seller carries out the repairs or deducts the fixing cost from the sale's value.

Run Your Numbers Once More

This is the final step in your due diligence. Using all of the data you have gathered above, now you need to run the numbers once more with the more elaborate data that you have obtained. Generating the information, you need to decide for the last time what the core objective of the process of due diligence is. It will help you determine if you should move on with the deal or not.

Here, you need to use the data available at your disposal to find out if the property will generate an acceptable revenue if you buy, rehab, and resell. If the potential for profit is acceptable to you, then you can move on with the deal. However, if it isn't, you need to check out other options.

Steps to Take if the Numbers Are Not Right

Hopefully, this won't be the case. However, there are times when you will notice that the numbers you come up with during the process of due diligence will show that the deal is not as good as it seemed at the agreed-upon price.

The way you deal with this situation has a huge role to play on if you plan to continuously make returns from flipping homes or make a profit only a few times. In some cases, house flippers get attached to deals and go ahead with them even when the numbers are not right. During these kinds of situations, all they are doing is postponing the challenges that arise with going through with a bad deal.

So, if you find out after your due diligence that the numbers are not right, what options are available to you? Check them out below:

Request for a Reduction in Price

Heading back to the seller and asking for a reduction in price is your initial course of action. Most times, being honest can make things go smoother. Reach out to the seller and inform them that your numbers are not right, and request they offer you support for your findings.

For instance, if you observed a list of hidden issues that require repairs during the process of due diligence, you can provide the seller with a list. In many situations, if you can prove to the seller that your new information during the process of due diligence that has an impact on the deal, they will be eager to consider reducing the price. If it is an REO deal, the bank will often need contractor bids or inspection reports before they will deliberate on a reduction of rates based on issues that came up during the process of due diligence.

Walk Away from The Deal

If you are unable to get a reduced price on the deal, you may have to walk away from the agreement. Your agent, contractors, and sellers may be unhappy, but this would be much better than investing in a property that would bring you no revenue.

If your due diligence comes out with great results, then you can go ahead with the project. If you do your due diligence the right way and hire the wrong contractor, you may still end up dealing with losses. The next chapter outlines the steps involved in hiring contractors.

Chapter 11: Hiring Contractors

You have put most of what you need in place, and now it is time for you to build another vital team: the team of contractors who will have the responsibility of getting you a decent profit for your investment. Great contractors are those who will transform your property from inhabitable to ready to sell.

However, you need to understand that finding a team of contractors with skills you can rely on is one of the most complex aspects of this business. The truth is, the number of great contractors is much lower than the unreliable ones. This is something that is not inevitable in the industry. Anyone can name himself as a contractor after buying a bunch of tools, and that makes the field saturated with numerous unskilled contractors.

How can you ensure you don't fall into the hands of unscrupulous workers and ensure you don't drown in unnecessary delays and hassles? This is what we will be covering in this chapter. Before going any further, you need to determine the kind of contractor you require for your project.

What Type of Contractor Do You Need?

Depending on the kind of project you want to work on, the following are contractors you may have to hire:

- General Contractor: This is one who oversees all areas of a project, like obtaining building permits, hiring and managing subcontractors, and setting appointments for inspections.

- Architect: An individual who deals with core renovations and designs homes. They are especially handy when your project involves alterations to the structure of a home.

- Specialty Contractor: These help in the installation of specific products like bathroom fixtures, and kitchen cabinets, among others.

- Build/Design Contractor: A contractor who offers both building and design services.

The majority of the time, your best bet will be to go with a general contractor as many of them can cover all other aspects of a project. Let's take a look at how you can find the right contractor for your project.

Finding the Right Contractor for Your Project

Hiring a general contractor can be of immense benefit to you. They are professionals in the field and can make constructive decisions on your behalf. For instance, if you want to make changes to a particular part of the home, your contractor would let you know whether it would lead to damage to the property or if it's a solid idea.

The general contractor largely supervises the project from the beginning to end without wasting any time, because their major role is to ensure the project goes smoothly. As opposed to doing it yourself, where you often make efforts to correct mistakes numerous times before you get it right, getting the services of a general contractor ensures the project goes right the first time.

Another benefit of hiring a general contractor is their capacity to help you develop a financial plan, which can keep the project going until it is over. They can let you know the cost of material and how much you will need to pay laborers. They will also let you know the timescales of a project, all of which are only possible because of the vast field of experience they have.

As a professional, a contractor is knowledgeable of the permits you need in various kinds of property renovations. This will ensure you don't get into legal trouble, as if you fail to obtain a necessary permit, you will be held liable and not the contractor. A contractor can also determine the aspects of the jobs they can take part in even if there is no available permit. With this, your project will always be ongoing and drawing closer to completion.

Places to Find Your Contractor

If you are in search of a contractor, here are some resources to consider:

Referrals from Real Estate Investment Clubs (REIC)

Contractors are always on the move or getting some work done. They do not remain in a location holding for people to hire them. One of the best places to begin is your reliable local REIC. The investors who are present in these meetings will likely be able to refer you to a decent contractor. And since you can be confident they have collaborated with them beforehand, you can rest assured that the contractors will have an excellent track record. The kinds of connections you make here can prove to be of immense benefit to you.

Ask Subcontractors

Next, if you know other fantastic sub-contractors, you can ask which general contractors they have collaborated with previously who they can endorse. Skilled subcontractors love partnering with great general contractors, so they usually have an idea of which contractors are efficient and which are not.

Check Out Your Farm Area

Taking a drive or walk around your farm area to look for contractors doing some work close-by is another means of finding contractors. Pull over or stop and begin a conversation. It offers you an opportunity to see how they carry out their projects and the kind of services they render in real-life scenarios.

Check Hardware Stores

You can locate general contractors at a Home Depot or other home improvement store. They are easy to spot once you are inside because they would be the ones purchasing a reasonable amount of supplies for rehabbing homes. The same as before, approach them and strike up a conversation.

Check Online

If you want something straightforward, the internet remains your best bet. Sometimes, all you need to do is run a search online for local contractors to find one close to you. To take it a step further, search Craigslist ads or ads on similar platforms where you can find contractors close to you. The only downside of this method is that you may find a lot of unskilled talent and may need to do a lot of work in choosing the most reliable worker. If you don't have many other options, though, this is a great way to begin.

Get a feel of them over the phone and go with your gut. Request references which you will be able to reach out to and ask them to show you the projects they have finished. Once you are through with the initial stage of finding a group of contractors you think would be great for the job, you will need to further narrow your options to the best candidates by asking them a few questions.

Questions to Ask Before You Hire a Contractor

It usually is less challenging to locate an individual that has worked for another investor previously. These individuals will understand that with you, they have the benefit of repeat work. By working with you, there is a possibility that they may not need to continually compete for jobs.

That being said, with this knowledge, the following are questions you need to ask a contractor before you hire:

Have You Worked for Someone Similar?

First, you need to ask if they have previously worked for someone in the house flipping business. If their response is yes, ask the number of jobs they have completed and the type of work done on those projects.

How Long Have You Been in This Job?

You need to find out how long the contractor has been in the field. As judgmental as it may seem, what you want is someone who has had ample experience in the field. This would mean they would be able to deal with any problem that arises. They will also have an understanding of the permits you need to make sure you don't fall into legal hitches.

Do You Work Alone?

You need to find out if they work without extra hands. There are benefits and drawbacks to this. A contractor who has helpers would be more expensive, but work progress would be faster. One without helpers may not cost as much, but work progress might be slowed. They are both good options, so long as you have weighed the benefits and drawbacks.

Supposing they do work with people, ask how many people they have on their team. If they have a small team, the contractor would not be an ideal option for a huge rehab project.

Is There Any Area You Don't Work On?

Ask if there is a specific part of the job they don't do. Can they work on plumbing and electrical? How about framing and roofing? You need to determine beforehand if there are areas they are uncomfortable working on. You don't want to incur additional expenses by hiring a contractor who does not do specific jobs and end up hiring someone else to fill in those blanks. It's best to go with someone versatile who can handle all aspects of a given project.

Are You Presently Working On Any Project?

This is an essential question to work. Rehab takes time, and the quicker you close, the faster you get your returns. If the contractor is busy with other projects, find out when they will be through. You don't want your project to be on hold for a few months, pending when a contractor will be free. What you need is someone who can begin as soon as possible.

Do You Have the Required License?

A license is vital and shows the level of skill and dedication a contractor has to their profession. However, in some areas, you can overlook this. If you are not doing an extensive rehab, a license may not be essential. Some contractors don't have a license but will have associates they can get these from if the need arises. However, if you want to be on the safe side, it is best to go with a licensed contractor.

Do You Have Insurance?

This is another very significant question. You need to find out if your contractor is insured. In the event of an injury, while working on your property, hospital bills can consume a whole lot of funds you could have used for other things. The same is also applicable in case there is damage to your property while working.

There are a few essential insurance coverages a contractor should have which include:

- Personal liability

- Property damage coverage

- Worker's compensation

Do not forget to request copies of current insurance certificates. With the right insurance you are indemnified from all the charges that may arise during the process of working on your project. There are a few things you may not find out from asking questions, and you can determine these by watching out for a few signs.

Signs to Look Out for When

Choosing a Contractor

- If a contractor offers you a price much lower than it should be or less than other bids, you need to be careful. Sometimes, cheaper is not better. Many times, contractors who have not been working for a while will require your job to pay their pending bills, individuals they owe or just to complete past projects they have already begun. This is a regular occurrence, and you need to exercise caution.

- Other times, shady contractors will inform you that they don't have sufficient funds to finish your job and require another deposit. The challenge with this could be that you have already settled them for your job, but the funds were channeled somewhere else. They will go down a slope and pull you in with them.

- Watch out for contractors who will try to appeal to your emotions by telling you a sad story in a bid to give them the job. It is okay to feel bad for them, but keep in mind that you are running a business and if your gut screams *NO!* you need to move on to the next candidate.

- Stay away from the ones who appear to

have substance abuse problems. If you come across a contractor who smells like a brewery or has erratic behavior indicative of drug use, you will want to move on to your next option. When picking a contractor you need someone in the right frame of mind, as errors can be very costly during a rehab project.

• Hiring a contractor without insurance is a horrible idea. The moment you find out they have no insurance, move on to the next candidate.

• Next, you need to stay away from contractors who request half the payment in advance. Many rehabbers have fallen into this trap and are left with a contractor who refuses to show up until you make numerous calls to them. Other times, they never even show up at all, and it would be a hassle to get your money back. Note that this method may work for some people, but if you are working with a contractor for the first time, it might be a good idea to avoid this scenario.

• Lastly, stay away from the ones who brag a lot. This may seem awkward, but in numerous cases, those who have a constant need to remind you of how great they are at their jobs are often anything but. Sometimes, contractors brag to prep you for the huge bid they are about to make. If you come across one who boasts a lot, move on to someone else.

Get Numerous Bids

Hold on for the bids to come falling in and try your best not to involve yourself in games. Some contractors will want to draw out information to determine what the others are bidding or tell you to state your price. Do all you can to avoid this and request that they all provide their bids. It is vital for you to have a scope of work in place, showing in detail the job you want to do to make things easier.

Speak to the candidates left and decide on the one you prefer the most after considering all the costs. If you made it evident to them that you would be offering lots of work opportunities, the bid they provided should be well within their comfort zone and yours. Even if you are okay with the price, try to engage in a little negotiation with every one of them and see what happens. As a rule of thumb, always ensure you negotiate even if you can only cut down the bid a little. You don't want the contractor feeling like they could have gotten much more.

Analyze the Job

Once you have chosen your contractor and they
have begun to work on the project, you need to watch
them closely. Watch how he works and note anything
you are not okay with. Some people act their best when
bidding for a job, but the instant they get it, they begin
to do the opposite of what they offered. This is why it is
very crucial to watch closely. If you are not satisfied with
the way a contractor works, what can you do?

What to Do About an Unreliable
Contractor

If your chosen contractor fails to meet his end of the
bargain in an agreement, you are within your rights to
terminate the contract. You don't have to keep up with
issues to prevent confrontation. Some contractors are
experienced at testing boundaries and would push you
to your limits. And once they observe that you won't
confront them, they will keep doing as they please
knowing they can get away with it.

When things are not going as they should, you need
to set things right. Do not keep enduring in the hopes
that things will get better, because the truth is that it
hardly ever does. Request corrections if something is not
going the way it should. This may be difficult, but it is an
essential step you need to take once you notice any

problems.

Understand Your Options of Payment

When working with contractors, you need to understand the payment options available to you. These tips can help:

- Avoid paying in cash: For projects that are not too big, you can pay via credit card or check. Lots of individuals make arrangements for financing to pay for more significant projects.

- Place a limit on down payment: There are laws in specific states that restrict the amount of cash a contractor can ask for as a down payment. Reach out to your local or state consumer agency to learn about the laws in your region.

- Make efforts to provide payments in milestones upon completion of clearly stated amounts of work. In doing this, if the work is not progressing as it should, contractors would not get payments on time as well. One more thing which is as important as understanding your payment options is your contract.

Draw Up a Written Contract

Different states have varying contract requirements. Even if it is not essential to draw up a written agreement in your place of residence, you need to request one. It should be concise, clear, detailed, and should consist of all the project essentials. Before signing any contract, make sure it includes the following:

- The name, phone number, license number, and address of the contractor

- A projected start and finish date

- The schedule of payment for the contractor, suppliers, and subcontractors

- The obligation of the contractor to get all the permits required

- How the contractor will deal with change orders. A change order is an authorization to the contractor, put down in writing, for them to make changes alongside the work defined in the main contract, and could have an impact on the project's schedule and cost.

- Information regarding warranties that cover workmanship and materials, as well as the addresses and names of the individuals who will honor them; in this case, this could include the manufacturer, contractors, and distributors. The warranty length and other restrictions should be clearly stated.

- The roles of the contractor and things they are not obligated to do. For instance, is cleaning up the site a part of the price? Request for a broom clause, which holds the contractor liable for all tasks related to cleaning, including stains and spills.

- An elaborate outline of all the materials, including every product's size, model, cost, and brand. If there are materials to be selected later on, the contract should indicate the individual charged with picking each item and the amount of money allocated to it.

- A statement of your right to revoke the contract within three working days, if the contract was signed in your residence or any location that is not the permanent site of business of the seller.

After Hiring a Contractor

Hiring the contractor is only the first step. After hiring, there are a few things to do to ensure your collaboration runs smoothly.

Keep detailed records

Ensure all the paperwork that has to do with your project is in one location. The paperwork may include:

- Change orders

- Copies of contract

- History of every payment (you may require receipts for tax purposes).

- All communications with your home improvement professionals

You may also want to keep a journal or record of all of your discussions, actions, and phone calls. You may also need to take pictures as progress is made on the project. These records are essential, especially if issues arise with your job during the construction process or after.

Release Payments Wisely

Do not complete the final payment until you are pleased with the work. In addition to being pleased with the tasks completed, it is vital to find out if suppliers and subcontractors have been settled, as well. Your state laws may give them the capacity to file a mechanic's lien against your property to fulfill any pending bills, compelling you to let go of your home to get them made whole. Look out for yourself by requesting the contractor, and all suppliers and subcontractors, sign a lien waiver or lien release.

Be Aware of the Limit for the Final Bill

There are local or state laws that restrict the amount the final fee can go beyond the estimate unless the increase has been approved by you. Look into these laws so you can be prepared.

Know When You Can Deny Payment

If you have issues with the services or items charged to a credit card, and you have tried to sort things out with the seller, you are within your rights to reach out to the company operating your credit card to deny payment for the services or items. You will be able to withhold payment up to the remaining amount of credit for the purchase, alongside any finance or associated charges.

Take Advantage of a Sign-Off Checklist

Before making the final payment, ensure that the following conditions have been met:

- All tasks are in accordance with the standards stated in the contract

- You have warranties in writing for workmanship and materials

- You have evidence that payment has been made to suppliers and subcontractors

- The work site has been cleared and cleaned up of surplus materials, equipment, and tools

- You have reviewed and accepted the work done

After getting your team of contractors in place, and work has kicked off on your property, you need to learn proper management to ensure everything goes as it should. Move on to the next chapter to learn how to do this efficiently.

Chapter 12: Managing Your Rehab

If you have gotten this far, it means you have most of what you need in place. However, even if you got the services of an excellent contractor, you may still need to manage the project to ensure everything goes as it should. When it comes to projects, the art of efficient project management is essential.

Any delay in the completion of a project, even as little as a day, means extra costs for you. So your goal should be to ensure you complete a project as quickly as possible without compromising quality. If you have a lot of people working for you, it is another compelling reason to complete projects fast. Presuming you have a team of 3 working on your project, whom you pay $20 per hour, that could add up to $400 daily. This means, for each day your project, you spend an additional $400, not including any other expenses. This makes it vital to complete projects as fast as prudently possible.

To ensure the project goes as it should, you need to have your scope of work in place and create a project schedule. Don't wait until you have closed a deal before putting these together. You need to have an idea of what you plan on doing and the costs it will entail before you sign any contract. As we covered earlier, the moment you have the property under contract, you need to do your due diligence and make sure you have a thorough understanding of all you need to do.

With that in mind, how do you make sure you manage your project effectively? Here are the things you need to put in place and do.

Make a detailed plan

Before you do any work, ensure you have already finalized your design. Instead of designing on the go, the rehab process is smoother when you don't have to make continuous changes. If you have no plan in place, you may see that available options are limited depending on the work that has been done already.

Weeks before the project, take some time to draw up plans, outline your specifications, and ensure you have made every decision before you move on. This will help you save money and time as you go on, and would drastically minimize the level of frustration for everyone involved in the project.

Don't Assume

When putting together a plan, don't assume any other involved party will understand your vision for the project except as it is explicitly stated. Put down every detail, even to the most seemingly irrelevant one. It is better to seem fussy than to be left with preventable mistakes that lead to disputes later on in the project.

For instance, if the bathroom will not be appealing if you use a specific color, ensure you state the color you want. If you don't specify what you want, you can't expect to see it come to fruition during the project. To avoid this, list *everything*.

Prepare the Scope of Work

Some general contractors will manage all aspects of a project. However, many of them don't do things like plumbing or electrical. Also, if you are hiring subcontractors or other service providers, you will need to have a clear outline of the work they need to do and the work they can't do, which you will allocate to other vendors. So after creating a list of all the work that your project entails, you will have to determine who you are going to assign the tasks to. A typical way of doing this is as follows:

- Check out the utilities

- Demolition

- Structural repairs, if needed

- Flooring

- Painting

- General construction, which may include interior and exterior

- Appliances and other facilities

- Checking of systems

- Cleaning

This is a flexible one, which means you can shuffle things up as you see fit. For instance, if the weather is great, and the HVAC vendor is occupied for the next two days or more, you don't need to stop work, because your employees and contractors won't have any issues with the weather conditions while working on your property. Also, you can do two things on the list at the same time. Work in the interior can begin the same time you are trimming the trees. The key thing here is to have a plan in place showing who is going to do each task and listing all the vendors before you begin anything.

Make Sure You Are All in Agreement

The next step, after creating the scope of work is to ensure you are all on the same page. You need to provide a detailed copy of your specifications to each of the vendors and subcontractors. Talk to them about the specifications and see areas they may be able to offer better suggestions.

When they know beforehand what part of the property an additional toilet or bathroom would be located, for example, the builders will know to leave a bit of space for pipes and other plumbing materials before plastering everything. This prevents the extra mess of breaking down walls to allocate pipes.

Dealing with Service Providers

Sadly, many vendors tend to disappoint. If you are collaborating with a vendor who flakes on appointments and can't be relied on to meet a specific schedule, you may have to schedule someone else. Knowing this, try not to ask contractors for a particular date a project will be completed. Unexpected things tend to happen, and a project may take more time than anticipated.

Nonetheless, you will want to ensure things are scheduled as close as possible without any complications. If there are occasions where two vendors can do their task simultaneously, don't hesitate to do it. You want to keep them as tightly scheduled as you can. For instance, plan the flooring shortly after construction and so on.

A good idea would be to use project management software or a spreadsheet to create a plan for everything, and monitor the completed tasks, list what needs to be scheduled and what has already been scheduled. This is vital because forgetting to do something minor during the construction stage may cause a long delay that could have been avoided from the start.

Do Not Alter Your Decisions

During a rehab, your contractor or builder may have many questions as work is ongoing. Some questions you may have to address include:

- Where should I put these lights?

- What color should be here?

The easiest way to deal with this is to consider as many of these questions as you can beforehand and have a response for them. Better still, let the information be in your specifications. When you are under pressure, you could begin to act on impulse, which might lead to regret later on. Taking too much time, on the other hand, can cause a delay in the project, which will cost you money and time down the road.

It is impossible to avoid questions you did not plan for, but anywhere possible, request that your contractors give you time to decide, without any delay to the project. It is fine to ask for their opinion, but do not choose under pressure.

Have a Contingency in Place

Even after you have planned as best as you should, there may be times when problems that you could not have seen coming, would crop up during your project. It is a great idea to have a plan B in your budget to accommodate issues like these, especially in a building that is quite old. You never can tell what condition you would find the walls when you tear up the kitchen cabinets.

In situations like this, you need to have a contingency in place instead of been thrown off your tracks when issues like these occur. Weigh the options available and make a decision. Your contractors would be able to advise you on the step to take, so take advantage of their experience and find the best course of action.

Don't Pay Contractors for Work Before Completion

Many new rehabbers have fallen into this trap and paid the total sum before the job even began. Most times, they lose their money as the contractor leaves town with the cash and never answers their phone again. Some are lucky and can get their work completed after incessant calls to the contractor, but the damage has already been done as the work takes twice the time it should have.

To prevent this, you need to make payments in milestones. For instance:

- 15% of the money up front to begin

- 1/3 of the balance paid after completing 1/3 of the task

- 1/3 of the balance after completing 2/3 of the job

- Final payment after finishing the work and you are satisfied

Ensure You Are Physically Present

This may not be needed if you are working with a team you trust. However, if you are not going to be present at the property throughout the process, ensure you pay surprise visits every few days.

Many rehabbers make the mistake of telling their contractor the exact time they will be checking in on them. If you are working with a good contractor, this may not be an issue. However, with an unscrupulous contractor, you just armed him with the information he needs to slow down his pace or go do something else during your project time.

Many contractors overbook themselves and will do all they can to complete two jobs simultaneously. This will end up reflecting one or both projects they are dealing with at that moment, all in a bid to make extra cash. You want to make sure that your contractors are not slacking off when you are not present, and they are moving ahead with your task.

Your best bet is to pay surprise visits to your work site without any consistency. If you are unable to go for these surprise checks, you can send in a relative or close friend to help you out with this once in a while as the project is ongoing. This will ensure contractors are always on their toes and channeling all their energy into completing your project.

Know Your Suppliers

There are house flippers who take charge of everything, right down to materials. On the other hand, some rehabbers delegate the tasks to the contractor so they don't have to deal with the stress. The decision lies with you to pick which option you are okay with.

However, you need to understand that contractors will typically choose cheaper materials if you leave it to them. For minor things, this may be fine, but when it has to do with the vital elements in the home like faucets and appliances, you won't want to choose based solely on price.

A better option would be to have a go-to depot that you have a personal rapport with, and get them to deliver the essential materials at a specific time and leave your contractor to supply the less critical materials.

Hire an Expert

Managing the project on your own can be rewarding, but there are specific skills you need. You need to be confident, strategic, organized, and able to deal with pressure. Also, you need to have time on your hands to supervise the work, which may be impossible if you have other things to do.

If you have the extra cash to invest, you can go the easy way and hire a project manager to do the work for you. It's better to spend more money and get the results you desire than to invest your time and money, battle with stress, and still be left with a poorly done project.

When you are through with the management of your rehab, the ideal result should be a finished project waiting to be sold. The next decision you will have to make after this is to choose between going with an agent or selling FSBO. More on this in the next chapter.

Chapter 13: Agent Versus FSBO

Selling a home is not easy, nor is it rocket science if you know what you are doing. It requires a lot of dedication, time, and hard work, and to save funds, lots of owners do it by themselves. There are benefits and drawbacks to selling a property without the help of a licensed real estate agent, and in the long run, only you can decide the best course of action for your home.

With this in mind, this chapter will be discussing the differences between both options to help you make a choice.

Is it Compulsory to Hire Real Estate Agents?

There is no law binding you to hire a real estate agent when it comes to selling homes. However, agents may be able to access information you won't be able to such as the MLS. If you decide to work with an agent, they will handle a huge chunk of the work ranging from pricing, listing, drawing up paperwork, among others.

FSBO or For Sale by Owner: What Does it Mean?

Sale by owner is when the owner of a property lists it without using a licensed real estate agent. If you decide to take this route, you will handle the entire process of selling the home, from beginning to end.

Agent vs. FSBO: Fees

Many investors who support FSBO choose to sell their properties FSBO because they believe it will save them cash. However, it was observed in a study done by Northwestern University, that of all the properties sold FSBO in Madison, Wisconsin got no less than the same amount of cash as properties sold by licensed agents.

Yes, agents do earn a commission from the sale price of the home, but these fees are channeled to the money and time needed to sell a home. If you decide to sell on your own, you will have to spend money to list the property, host prospective buyers, and stage, all of which require cash.

On the other hand, real estate agents will help take pictures of your home, stage, and list it on the MLS, which can only be accessed by agents. If you collaborate with an agent, you won't need to pay the fees involved in listing a home. Real estate agents will also host property viewings and open houses by themselves, which means you can concentrate on other activities. Also, if you sell FSBO, you will still have to pay some agent's fees.

Marketing

You need the right buyers for a successful home sale. As stated in a study carried out by the National Association of Realtors, 90 percent of individuals who wanted to purchase homes searched online. Real estate agents have the MLS and other methods of getting visibility both online and offline. In contrast, as an FSBO seller, you can buy ads in newspapers or using online social media platforms.

Time

The longer a property stays on the market, the less the potential selling price. It was observed by the National Association of Realtors that properties sold via the MLS, sold 20 days quicker on average, while 20 percent of the listings done FSBO had to re-renewed because they were unable to sell.

There is a lot of time involved in scheduling property viewings, staging, and getting offers on a home. Agents invest a lot of time, sometimes during holidays and often during weekends to ensure that the house sells for the appropriate amount as fast as possible. If you have a full-time job and decide to sell FSBO, you may need to cut down your work hours to do home showings, which means a reduction on your paycheck as well. Even if you don't work full time, are you ready to invest all of your time in showings and marketing? Would you be willing to drop all you are doing to meet up with a prospective buyer when they want to see a home?

If you are unable to do all of these, your home may spend more time on the market, and many buyers see this as a red flag even if you have a good reason for it.

Negotiation

Selling a home is a legal deal. For this reason, you will have to negotiate with buyers. If you turn over this role to a real estate agent, they will deal with negotiations on your behalf. However, as an FSBO seller, you would need to do the negotiations on your own. A real estate agent typically negotiates with the buyer's attorney, agent, the buyer themself, and the bank appraiser. The experience the real estate agent has underneath their belt makes all of these a breeze for them. However, if you sell FSBO, you will need to do the strategizing on your own and depend on your skills and expertise, which may not yet be developed, especially as a new seller.

Even investors with lots of experience stick to using agents. This is because they sell homes for a living, and know the inner workings of selling a home. They understand how the market in your environment works and are professionals when it comes to selling homes. Real estate agents sell two to four homes weekly, which is a record you may not be able to beat anytime soon.

Legal Assistance

The sale of a home is a legitimate deal. If you choose to sell your property on your own, some states would not authorize you to go through the process of closing without the presence of a real estate agent. Also, unless you understand legal documents, you may miss some vital piece of information when signing a contract and be left with a lawsuit later on.

An experienced agent understands all the legal workings of selling a home and can aid in ensuring you don't have to deal with a lawsuit later on.

Which Is the Ideal Option For You?

Selling FSBO should be the last option on your list when you want to sell a home. The benefits offered by a real estate agent outweighs the drawbacks you face when selling FSBO. Nevertheless, the final decision lies with you, and whether you believe you can handle all the risks involved. Only you know the best course of action for your business.

Chapter 14: Staging

If you want the sale of your home to be quicker, staging it lets you show it in its best look, inspiring potential buyers to view themselves residing there. It enables you to stay ahead in a competitive market, as buyers of homes are getting used to seeing staged homes, both in online listings and in person.

Staging A Home: What Does it Mean?

At its core, staging has to do with the enhancement of an item, thereby making it more appealing to buyers, which in turn boosts its value. If you head to a store, you would be more likely to pay more if the product comes in a nice package and it is displayed in a nice way. If it seems to be in poor condition, you may not want to pay as much. The same is applicable when selling a property.

Home staging has to do with preparing your property for the market and marketing its selling points. You do this by creating an emotional and visual appeal which will pull in buyers, to imagine what life in that home would be like. Buying a home is an emotional decision as well as a financial one. The buyer must have the capacity to envision themselves residing in the home, living the lifestyle portrayed by the home, to create the craving to buy that house. You need to understand that even though the property you did your best to fix and flip is an investment to you – *you* need to make buyers feel like the home is the ideal one for *them*.

Does Staging Work?

Buyers are more responsive to staged homes in comparison to those that are not properly staged. If you fail to stage your home, you are only giving way for the competition to sell quicker than you and losing the opportunity to put more money in your pockets.

Staging has become a final touch for getting your home ready for the market. It also allows you to get the highest price for your home in the shortest amount of time.

Now that you understand the benefits of staging your home, let's check out a few hints to help you stage your home the right way:

Use Neutral Colors

This may cost you more cash and time, but it can help make a huge difference when it comes to getting your home off the market for the best price. Bright colors are great for people who want to show their personalities in their own home; however, for many buyers, it can be a serious turn-off.

The best things you can do for your home when staging it is to paint it using neutral colors like white and gray. Using loud colors can distract potential buyers from some crucial selling point of the home. Many buyers may love bright colors, but using neutral colors in the home will offer them the choice when it comes to doing so or not.

Clean and Clean Some More

This is common knowledge, but it is something lots of rehabbers miss. When you are placing your home on the market, the first thing to do is to clean it like never before. You want every part of the house to glisten.

A clean home tells a buyer that it is well taken care of. If there were certain areas you missed during the rehab, now is the time to make sure you clean all of it as best you can.

Keep Things Fresh

Placing too many extra items in the home can make it look cluttered. However, a few fresh, strategically placed flowers and plants can add some freshness and life to the house. Let them be properly spaced out, so they don't clutter a specific area, but ensure you place some fresh items in key areas.

Try to place some bright flowers or a little potted plant in the living room or kitchen center table. If you are not a fan of fresh plants, you can use fake plants, as they perform the same role and last longer.

Another way of keeping things fresh is to ensure the home has no odor. A deep clean can help eradicate any smells left behind from the rehab, but you need to ensure there is no lingering odor that can welcome buyers during a showing. You could use some air fresheners or scented oils to make rooms smell more pleasant to buyers. Even so, remember not to overdo it as very strong smells, no matter how pleasant, can be a turn-off to most people, especially those with a sensitive sense of smell.

Let There Be Light

Dark rooms have a sad aura to them. Most buyers would prefer seeing bright rooms. This means lighting is a vital aspect of home staging. You can brighten up a room by allowing as much light as possible to shine in the home.

An easy way to do this is to open all the window blinds. In addition to bringing in more light, it will make the room look bigger to potential buyers. Make sure all the lights in the home are turned on during a showing, including lights in closets and lamps. It will ensure the house seems more welcoming and help the buyer figure out where to go next. Make sure you have appealing light fixtures, and if you have dingy or old-looking lampshades, try replacing them — toy around with numerous lighting types and temperatures to get the most alluring one.

First Stage the Vital Rooms

Staging the whole home is not a bad idea; nevertheless, if you don't have the time, begin by staging the essential parts of the house. The living room is the most important part when it comes to staging as this is the first place most buyers see when they head into a home. Next should be the master bedroom and then the kitchen. Additional bedrooms should be last on your list during a staging.

Rent Some Furniture

When renting furniture, you don't want to overdo it. A home with less furniture will look more appealing and larger to many buyers.

When the furniture comes in, position chairs, table, and couches from the wall, this is an approach known as "floating" the furniture. Ensure the space is anchored with an area rug as it helps in creating an intimate and comfortable space, great for having conversations with friends and family.

You want to ensure you have ample space to walk around. It aids buyers in navigating the space and assists them in imagining their personal furniture in every room.

Don't Ignore the Curb

If the exterior of the property is not appealing enough, you probably won't get as many buyers as you should into the home. By making the curb appeal go up, you can draw more potential buyers into the home.

You can achieve this by following these tips:

- Wash the walkways and house

- Ensure your windows are clean

- Trim down overgrown shrubs and mow the lawns

- Plant beautiful flowers

- Make the house number is not difficult to read

- If there is a porch, add outdoor furniture

- Place potted plants and a welcome mat on your doorstep

Staging a home does not mean you have to spend a lot of cash. Instead, you need to make wise decisions. Once you have done everything in your power to show your home in the best manner possible, all that is left is to wait for the appropriate buyer to step in and get yourself ready for the closing process.

Chapter 15: The Closing

Process

If this is your first time selling or buying a home, this can be a scary process. Not only do you need to get the timing right, but you also have a lot of work to do to ensure it is a successful transaction. If you are working alongside an agent, things may be a little easier, but you need to understand how to get the best of a deal as well.

Also, you need to understand how you can ensure you complete the sale promptly. So you don't waste your money and time during the process. We will be covering all of this in the next few pages. But first, let's see what closing means.

What Is a Closing?

Closing is the process whereby the house seller and buyer satisfy all of the promises made in the sales contract. It typically has to do with the transfer of documents and money so that you, as the seller, can transfer control and ownership of the property clear and free to the buyers. In addition to this, you will clear up all the remaining loans on the house and settle up with all the parties who helped in expediting the sale and closing.

Having covered this, let's take a look at what the closing process is like for you as a seller.

House Closing Process for Sellers

Negotiating

When a buyer makes you an offer, you are left with three choices:

- You can accept the terms if you find them suitable

- You can make a counteroffer and alter a few of the terms

- You can refuse the offer and walk away

You need to try to determine what inspires a buyer to purchase your property. If you know this, you will have the ability to negotiate terms aside from price. You can make them pay fees that would usually be yours to pay and ask them to cover specific repairs that may be found in an inspection. There are numerous ways you can get a great deal out of a sale without altering the price.

Don't let your emotions cloud your judgment during a negotiation. It is just business, and nothing is personal.

You may still need something from a buyer before you close, and you don't want an angry buyer on your hands.

If you have many offers, you can play them off each other. Let all prospective buyers know that someone is offering higher and offer them the opportunity to alter their prices. Schedule a time and date for when you will accept the best offers. Anyone who has a serious interest in your property will provide feedback fast.

Take your time during negotiations but know that you have to create a balance, as you don't want it dragging on for too long. This aspect of the closing process should not take longer than three days. Going beyond this can make a buyer lose interest.

Closing Costs

For you as a seller, closing costs can add up for the buyer and yourself when you transfer the real estate title. You will need to pay title fees, closing fees, a part of the transfer taxes and all real estate taxes that have gathered and not been paid during the period of ownership.

Be ready to take responsibility for paying escrow fees, recording fees, lien releases, and repair fees, among others. Fees differ based on the state so you may be unable to provide a proper estimate for them but note that these costs can really add up. If you are working with a real estate agent, request that they provide an estimate of all the closing costs from the start. Note what the estimate consists of, so you can negotiate with prospective buyers as regards contingencies.

Agent Percentage

If you added a real estate agent to your team, based on your location in the US, you pay them 5 -7 percent of what you sold your property for. You will have to find out what the right rate is for your location. The seller typically pays the commission of the agent, and if there are a selling and buying agent, they both share the commission.

You can negotiate with agents with regard to their commissions, but it is not usually a great idea. Agents will focus on properties they get more money from, so if your property pays an agent less, the agent might focus on selling off other properties on their listing with promises of higher commissions. It is best to pay an agent what they are due to ensure you have their attention. Better still, you can offer a bonus for when they sell the property, as doing this can help you get a quicker sale.

Buyer's Due Diligence

Similar to your due diligence, your buyers will also run due diligence on your property. The buyer's research is the same form of due diligence you run on a property before purchasing it, which we covered in Chapter 10. Its best to prepare yourself for any extra expenses you might incur.

Closing

As we covered earlier, closing is when the buyer offers cash to the seller in exchange for the deed of the property. The seller and the buyer have to be in the closing, with their attorneys (if needed), closing agent, and real estate agents. If you are not going to be in attendance with your attorney, make sure you prepare your closing documents beforehand. If this is your first close, ensure you go through all the documents with your lawyer before closing, so you understand what you want to sign and agree to.

A disbursement sheet which outlines the amount of money the buyer has to bring to the closing table and the amount the seller leaves with will be put in place. Ensure the provisions are accurate, and they follow the conditions of the agreement of sale. You need to ensure that you are being offered the entitlement you deserve.

After all, the documents have been signed, and the closing process is complete, ensure the amount of the cash you leave with tallies with what is owed to you on the disbursement sheet. If it fails to match, don't leave until it does. The disbursement sheet has to be accurate, as it is a legal record of the deal. The property's title history will already have been revised by the title agency you are working with, and with any luck, they will have cleared any pending issues with the title. The title agent will be responsible for ensuring the figures align, gathering needed signatures, authenticating, and issuing checks. Keep a positive relationship with your closer, as they can make sure the process of closing is as smooth as possible or can make it a very hectic experience. The title company will also have the responsibility of putting the deed of the property on record with the local government.

For a seller, the closing process can consume a lot of time, especially if you are not prepared. Putting in as much as you need beforehand and being aware of what to anticipate will make the experience seamless for all parties involved.

When Is Your Property Categorized as Sold?

Your property could be categorized as sold at any point during the closing process. Still, in theory, your home has not been sold until you no longer have ownership. Your property is sold after the deed has been transferred and the money collected. Once that has happened, pat yourself on the back. You can now consider yourself a successful first-time house flipper.

Conclusion

Congratulations! You have reached the end of what could well prove to be a very lucrative journey. Rehabbing homes comes with a variety of possibilities, but also carries a lot of risks. Knowing these risks and preparing for them ahead of time is half to battle.

Don't forget to make a detailed plan before you go into this business or you may find yourself discouraged when you face problems down the road. Planning, communicating, and doing thorough research are all key when it comes to the process of flipping homes.

I have offered you all the essential information you need. All you have to do is to read, assimilate, and apply what you have learned efficiently, so the whole process is seamless for you, for your first flipped home and hopefully many more to come.

9 781951 652241